CW00708751

To 'L'
all my love
from
'M'
xxx

Miss Lister of Shibden Hall

Selected Letters (1800-1840)

Anne Lister

MISS LISTER OF SHIBDEN HALL

Selected Letters (1800-1840)

Edited by

Muriel M. Green

The Book Guild Ltd.
Sussex, England

This book is sold subject to the condition that it shall not, by way of trade or otherwise, be lent, re-sold, hired out, photocopied or held in any retrieval system, or otherwise circulated without the publisher's prior consent in any form of binding or cover other than that in which this is published and without a similar condition including this condition being imposed on the subsequent purchaser.

The Book Guild Ltd.
25 High Street,
Lewes, Sussex.

First published 1992
© Muriel M. Green 1992
Set in Baskerville
Typesetting by Ashford Setting & Design,
Ashford, Middlesex.
Printed in Great Britain by
Antony Rowe Ltd.,
Chippenham, Wiltshire.

A catalogue record for this book is
available from the British Library.

ISBN 0 86332 672 2

CONTENTS

LIST OF ILLUSTRATIONS

CHRONOLOGY

1791 April 3   Anne Lister born at Welton, South Cave, in the East Riding of Yorkshire, the second child of Captain Jeremy Lister (who fought in the American War of Independence) and Rebecca Lister (née Battle). Their first child, John, born in 1789 died the same year.

1793   The family moved to Skelfler House, Market Weighton. A third child was born, Samuel, who became Anne's favourite relative.

1795   Another son, also called John, was born.

1798 May   Anne was sent to Mrs Hague and Chettles' school in Agnes Gate, Ripon, for about two years, because her parents found her an unmanageable tomboy.

1801 September   A third son, Jeremy, was born: he died in February 1802.

1801-1805   Anne was educated at home where the Rev. George Skelding was her tutor. On her frequent visits to her Uncle James and Aunt Anne, at Shibden Hall, she had lessons with the Misses Mellin.

1805   Anne became 'a parlour boarder', at the Manor House School, York, where Eliza

Raine, a beautiful coloured girl, the daughter of William Raine, a surgeon in the East India Company's service, became her devoted friend. She spent holidays with Anne at Market Weighton and at Shibden Hall. Anne began to keep a journal, covering 1806-1810: this account has not survived, but notebooks two and three, covering 1816-1817 are in the Lister Collection in the Calderdale Archives at Calderdale Central Library, Northgate, Halifax.

1806   Anne left the Manor House School, York, continuing her education under the Rev. Samuel Knight, Vicar of Holy Trinity Church, Halifax while living at Shibden Hall.

1808 June   Captain Lister decided to sell the Market Weighton estate and brought his family to Halifax where they lived at various addresses, including Northgate House which was part of the Shibden Hall estate.

1809-1810   Anne spent seven months with Mr William Duffin (a surgeon) and his wife at Red House, York, visiting also the Norcliffes of Langton hall, Malton.

1810 January   John Lister, aged fourteen, died.

1810-1815   Owing to 'disagreeables' at home, Anne spent most of this time paying visits to friends in York and Malton.

1815 May   Anne came to live with her uncle and aunt at Shibden Hall with whom she was much happier than with her parents.

1816	Her greatest friend, Mariana Belcombe, whom she had met in York in 1810, married Charles Lawton, of Lawton Hall, Cheshire.
1817	Anne began to keep her quarto volume journal (twenty-four volumes by 1840).
November 8	Anne's Uncle Joseph Lister died at Northgate House.
November 18	Her mother, Rebecca Lister died, aged c. forty-seven. Anne still studying with Mr Knight (classics and mathematics).
1818	Paid visits to the Norcliffes at Langton Hall, to Market Weighton, and to the Duffins at York.
1819	To Paris with her Aunt Anne for three weeks.
1820 February 21	Met Sibbella Maclean at York: she was to become another devoted friend.
1820-1821	Visits to friends, reading, and study.
1822 March	Partial sale of the Market Weighton estate.
July 11-27	Tour of North Wales with Aunt Anne, including a visit to the Ladies of Llangollen.
August 30	To Paris with her father and sister.
1823	To York: to Wharfedale with Aunt Anne — Scarborough, Langton and York.

1824 July 24-August 6	To the Lake District with her aunt.
August 24-March 1825	To Paris with her maid to improve her French, and to be cured of a virus infection.
1825 August 3-September 23	To Buxton with her aunt.
1826 January 26	Uncle James Lister of Shibden Hall died, leaving the estate to Anne, with a life interest for his sister, Anne Lister, senior.
May	Anne borrowed £2,000 for work on the Shibden Hall estate. Visits to Cheshire, Dublin, Oxford and London.
August 17	The two Miss Listers paid an almost two year visit to Paris, for the sake of their health. Anne attended lectures at the Collège de France.
1827 June-October	Anne Lister and her friend, Mrs Maria Barlow and daughter, Jane, toured Switzerland and Italy.
1828 March 17	The two Miss Listers left Paris.
May 19	Two months sight-seeing in Scotland with Sibbella Maclean. Supervising tree-planting and other work at Shibden Hall.
1829 February	Repaid the loan of £2,000.
April 12	To Paris with Vere Hobart. Attended lectures at Le Jardin des Plantes.

August 14	To Belgium with Vere Hobart and her grandmother, Lady Louisa Stuart.
September 16	Rhine tour with Lady Caroline Duff Gordon, and to the Netherlands.
December 31	Attended an Embassy Ball in Paris.
1830	Studying science — anatomy, mineralogy, etc. in Paris.
August 17-October 7	Trip to the Pyrenees with Lady Stuart de Rothesay and her children.
October 7-31	Travelling in the South of France.
November 16	Anne's great friend, Sibbella Maclean, died.
December-May 1831	Attending Cuvier's lectures in Paris.
1831 May 23	Anne and her aunt leave Paris.
August 4-17	To Holland with Mrs Mariana Lawton.
September 11	Journey on the newly opened railroad from Manchester to Liverpool and back.
September 15-30	Visiting friends in Hampshire and travelling to the Isle of Wight and Sussex.
November	Spent five months at St Leonards and Hastings with Vere Hobart.
1832 May-November	Travelling in Yorkshire; busy with estate affairs, elections, selling land, etc.
1833 January-May	Occupied with business relating to coal mines, quarries, etc.
July 17	Left London for Paris.

August 18	To Copenhagen with Mlle Ferrall, via the Netherlands, Germany, and then by sea.
September 18-November 30	Copenhagen — left hastily owing to Anne Lister senior's illness at Shibden.
December 16	Arrived in London.
1834	Anne arranged for a joint household with Ann Walker of Lightcliffe.
April 2-June 4	They toured Yorkshire together.
June 14-August 27	France and Switzerland with Ann Walker.
September	Ann Walker came to live at Shibden Hall.
November	Travelling to York, Hull, and by train to Leeds.
1835	Travelling to York, Kirkstall Abbey on a sketching expedition, London, Buxton, etc.
November	Opening new collieries at Shibden.
1836 April 3	Captain Jeremy Lister died.
October 10	Anne Lister, senior, died.
1837 January 3	Anne mortgaged Northgate Hotel and let it in November.
1838 May 2	To Brussels and Paris with Ann Walker.
June 20	To the Pyrenees for mountaineering.
November 27	Returned to Shibden. Busy with estate affairs, coal mines, financial difficulties.

1839 January **May**	Attending to the building of the West tower as a library — alterations to the main hall and gallery.
May	Chartist riots threatened.
1839 June 20	Anne and her friend Ann Walker left for a tour of Europe and Russia travelling via Dunkerque, Belgium, Germany, Copenhagen, Götteborg.
July 20- **September 14**	Through Sweden, Norway, Finland, and Russia.
September 26- **October 7**	At St Petersburg.
October 12- **February 4 1840**	Moscow: then on to Astrakhan, Kislyar in the Caucasus — Tiflis — Baku (May 16-26).
June 28-July 9	Koutais and district until returning to Koutais on July 27 and travelling further to Zugdidi and Djkali on August 11 when the journal ends.
September 22	Anne Lister died at Koutais.

Chief people referred to in the Letters.

Captain Jeremy Lister)
Rebecca Lister   )   parents of Anne Lister.

   their children Samuel, John and Marian.

James Lister, of Shibden Hall, brother of Captain Jeremy Lister) uncle and aunt
Anne Lister (senior)   sister of Captain Jeremy Lister   ) of Anne Lister.

Jeremy Lister = Anne Hall

James Lister	Joseph Lister	Jeremy Lister = Rebecca Battle	Martha Lister	Anne Lister
1748-1826	1750-1817	1752-1836	1763-1809	1765-1836

John	Anne Lister	Ensign Samual Lister	John Lister	Marian Lister	Jeremy
1789	of Shibden Hall	1793-1813	1795-1810	1797-1882	1801-1802
	1791-1840				

Friends

William Duffin, surgeon, of York.
Mariana Lawton (née Belcombe), of Lawton Hall, Cheshire. ('Mary')
Mrs Ann Norcliffe and her daughters Isabella, Charlotte, Mary (later Mrs Best)
Eliza Raine, a schoolfriend at the Manor House School, York.
Vere Hobart (later Lady Vere Cameron) and her sister Lady Harriet de Hagemann.
Sibbella Maclean of Coll, Tobermory   )
Lady Louisa Stuart, the Lodge, Richmond Park.)   aunts of the above
Lord Stuart de Rothesay (son of Lady Stuart), British Ambassador in Paris
Lady E. Stuart de Rothesay, wife of Lord Stuart de Rothesay.
Lady Duff Gordon, and her son Cosmo.
Sophy Ferrall   )
Countess Blucher)   sisters
Mrs Maria Barlow of Guernsey.
Miss Ann Walker, of Lightcliffe, near Halifax (Adny).
The Rev. George Skelding, Anne Lister's tutor at Market Weighton.
The Rev. Samual Knight, Anne Lister's tutor in Halifax.

Samuel Washington   )
David Booth   )   stewards
George Playforth   coachman

Cameron   )
Cordingley   )
McDonald   )   maids
Eugénie   )

Caradoc, Hotspur and Percy (horses)

Shibden Hall in the early nineteenth century

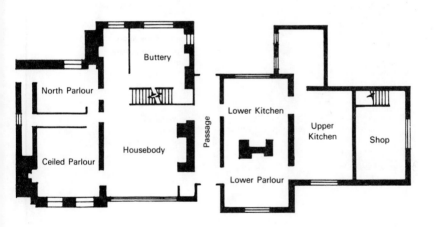

Adapted from the drawings by W.B. Trigg in Halifax Antiquarian Society Papers. 1926.

INTRODUCTION

During the three hundred years that the Lister family lived at Shibden Hall, Halifax, undoubtedly the most remarkable member was Miss Anne Lister, who was born on April 3 1791, and died in Russia on September 22 1840. Her journal (in twenty-four closely written quarto volumes) and her voluminous correspondence in the Calderdale Archives, Northgate, Halifax, show her to have been a woman of character and far in advance of her time. She was independent in thought and spirit, refusing slavishly to follow the fashions of the day. Her outlook was considered rather masculine in her time, when women were content to sit at home and mildly accept all the new ideas, without thinking of helping to put them into practice. Her mode of dress, her masculinity, and her rather eccentric behaviour amused her friends, and earned her the name 'Gentleman Jack' among the local populace.

Living as she did in the troublous time of the wars with France and America, the Luddite riots, the Parliamentary Reform agitation, and in the reign of four monarchs, she yet played an important part in the social history of Halifax. She was active in the spread of popular education at the time when the Mechanics' Institutes were emerging; she took an interest in all the educational institutions of the town — the libraries, museums, the Halifax Literary and Philosophical Society (of which, in the year 1831 she was the only woman member eligible for election on the committee).

Politics, too, engaged much of Anne Lister's attention; she helped considerably in the local elections, both with financial aid, and by visiting her tenants and influencing their votes. She had an astonishing business capacity and even during the lifetime of her uncle and aunt (with whom she lived for many years at Shibden Hall) she managed the estate, supervised building operations, looked after the legal interests and family matters, and, amid all these activities, she had time to set aside certain hours of the day for study, general reading, and letter writing.

Before the Listers' occupation of Shibden Hall (c.1619) it had been virtually in the hands of one family, the descent being on the female side. The Hall came into the Lister family by the marriages of Thomas and John Lister to two of the co-heiresses, Sybil and Phoebe Hemingway, in 1619 and 1625 respectively. The succeeding generations of Listers, included apothecaries, lawyers, schoolmasters and scholars. James Lister who inherited the property in 1788 left it to his favourite and very capable niece, Anne, rather than to his brother Captain Jeremy, as he feared the latter would leave it to his two daughters, Anne and Marian jointly which might result in the division of the estate. Anne Lister left a life interest to her friend, Ann Walker and on the latter's death (in 1853) Anne's cousin, Dr John Lister, of Swansea, who was a descendant of one of the Listers who went to Virginia in the eighteenth century, succeeded. During Dr Lister's residence at Shibden Hall (1853-1857) the coal-mines were not as prosperous as in Anne's day, and consequently the difficult task of maintaining the estate on a very diminished income was left to his son, John Lister, M.A. (1847-1933) a local historian, and writer on the early wool trade.

In August 1788 Captain Jeremy Lister married Rebecca Battle of Welton, in the East Riding of Yorkshire. The Captain was then thirty-five years of age while his bride was only eighteen. Their first child, John, was born in 1789 and died the same year. Anne was born on April 3 1791, at Welton. Two years later the Listers bought an estate, Skelfler House, at Market Weighton (East Riding), and there a third child, Samuel, was born in May 1793. A great friendship existed between Anne and Samuel and the sisterly advice in Anne's letters during the period he was an ensign in the army is often amusing. His early death by drowning, at the age of twenty, was a great sorrow to Anne. The Listers were singularly unfortunate with their male children; their fourth child, christened John after the first-born, was born in 1795 and was barely fifteen when he died of some childish complaint. The next child, Marian, was born in 1797 and outlived all the other members of the family; she died shortly before her eighty-fifth birthday, in 1882. Jeremy, the last child, was born in 1801 and died the following year.

Shortly after Anne's seventh birthday she was sent to Mrs Hague's and Chettle's school, in Agnesgate Ripon[1]. At this period she was 'a singular child, and singularly dressed, but genteel-looking, very quick and independent, and quite above telling an untruth; whistled very well; a great favourite of Mrs Chettle'. This description was afforded by a former schoolfellow, in 1822, and recorded in Anne's journal. She appears to have remained in this school until 1800, or possibly longer, and then was taught at home.

In 1802 and 1803 she visited her uncle and aunt, James and Anne Lister, at Shibden Hall, Halifax. The latter stay lasted nearly a year; her time-table shows that she continued her education, her teachers being Miss Sarah and Miss Grace Mellin, of Halifax.

When Anne returned to Market Weighton, in 1804, she had lessons with the Rev. George Skelding[2], Vicar of Market Weighton, until the following summer, when she was sent as 'a parlour boarder' to the Manor House School, York, which was one of the best girls' schools in the County. Here began her friendship with Eliza Raine, and it was probably during this period that she met Eliza's friends, the Duffins, of Red House, York.

Although Anne left school in 1800, she had by no means finished her education. On the contrary it appears from a letter dated May 26, 1825 (see page 84) that she did not begin to study seriously until she was well on in her teens. Her reading, however, had been wide and intelligent, providing her with a good store of general knowledge. She now began to study under the Rev. Samuel Knight, Vicar of Holy Trinity Church, Halifax.

On leaving school Anne began to keep a journal. The entries show that she joined in all the intellectual and cultural activities of Halifax. About this time Captain Lister and family were living in Halifax, because they found the upkeep of the Market Weighton estate too expensive: they were trying to find a purchaser for it. Anne, at this time, was staying with her uncle and aunt where she was always happier than at home where

---

[1] In 1822 this became the Mechanics' Institute.

[2] Rev. George Skelding (1737-1819)

she experienced many 'disagreeables'. She appears to have had little in common with her parents, apparently inheriting her intellectual gifts and love of learning from an earlier generation on her father's side of the family. Captain Lister had few interests, and apart from the fact that he fought with some distinction in the American War of Independence, and kept a diary of events, which was published in part, in 1931, by Harvard University[3], was quite undistinguished. Mrs Rebecca Lister seems to have been wholly taken up with her numerous children and her friends: in her later years she caused her family much unhappiness by her intemperance.

At the end of 1809 Anne went on a seven months' visit to the Duffins in York, where by this time she had a large circle of friends. During the next few years she also visited her friends the Norcliffes at Langton Hall, Malton (near York) and accompanied them to Bath. Much of this travelling was undertaken to avoid the unhappiness of home life, so when Anne returned to Halifax, in May 1815, it was with the decision to live permanently with her uncle and aunt at Shibden Hall. Here she was always very welcome, and of great assistance to Uncle James in the management of the estate.

An entry in Anne's journal, on May 17 1817, shows how she spent her time at this period, when she was twenty-six years of age:- '*I mean to proceed diligently, in the hope that, if I live, I may some time attain a tolerable proficiency in mathematical studies. I would rather be a philosopher than a polyglot, and mean to turn my attention eventually and principally to natural philosophy. For the present I mean to devote my mornings before breakfast to Greek, and afterwards, till dinner, to divide the time equally between Euclid and arithmetic, till I have waded through Walkingham[4], when I shall recommence my long neglected algebra. I must read a page or two of French now and then, when I can. The afternoons and evenings are set apart for general reading, for walking half-an-hour or three-quarters, (and) practice on the flute*'.

---

[3] *Concord Fight*, being so much of the Narrative of Ensign Jeremy Lister ... as pertains to his service on April 19, 1775, and to his experience in Boston during the early months of the Siege. 1931.

[4] The Tutor's assistant; being a compendium of arithmetic and a complete question-book in five parts, by Francis Walkingame: London 1751 (and other editions).

She expressed herself as 'disappointed and grieved' with herself if ever she stayed in bed after five a.m., and wrote further, '*I am well convinced my only chance of comfort is in rigorous and unrelaxed occupation of mind*'. She was still studying under the Rev. Samuel Knight.

A three weeks' visit to Paris, in 1819, with her aunt, was but an introduction to many continental tours. During their round of sight-seeing Anne made inquiries about studying in Paris which was a long cherished plan of hers. Several days were spent in London on the return journey and the two Miss Listers were indefatigable in visiting all the places of interest.

Social calls played an important part in Anne Lister's life in Halifax. She visited all the chief families — the Rawsons of Stoney Royde, the Edwards of Pye Nest, the Walkers of Lightcliffe, the Dysons of Willow Field, the Greenups of Darcey Hey, the Waterhouses of Well Head, and many others. She had an objection to parties, and her friends knew not to invite her if there would be any strangers present. There was evidently a little jealousy among the people who were unable to get an introduction to Miss Lister, and this gave rise to gossip about her small eccentricities — her masculinity, snobbishness, love of study, and her habit of keeping a journal in which they feared they might figure.

Besides her very detailed journal (the intimate parts of which were written in a crypt alphabet devised by herself), Anne kept accounts of all her expenditure, a record of all letters received and sent (and these amounted to several a day, in spite of the high postage rates in those days), a 'literary journal' showing the books she had read, and at times she made extracts from the book she was reading, as a typical entry in her diary (on April 28 1820) shows:- '*Sat up looking over Horace. I have taken a great fancy to him, and when I open him, know not how to put him away*'.

In addition to her social and literary activities Anne helped with the management of her uncle's estate. The early Tudor house and grounds were very dear to her, and she encouraged her uncle to buy old farms and property in the neighbourhood which had formerly belonged to the Shibden Hall estate. She was an astute business woman, capable of drawing up legal documents, negotiating purchases and sales. She superintended repairs to the farms and cottages, the planting and pruning of trees, the making of paths and roads on the estate, and the

Shibden Hall, the fifteenth century home of Anne Lister

working of the coal-mines which, in the nineteenth century, were at the height of their prosperity.

Ever since Mrs Rebecca Lister's death, in 1817, Captain Lister had been trying to sell his estate at Market Weighton, so as to be able to live in a smaller way. In February 1822 his daughter, with characteristic energy, arranged an interview with a London estate agent, and personally conducted him round the estate. This resulted in its sale in the summer whereupon Captain Lister and Marian came to stay at Shibden Hall until they found a house in Halifax.

The next few years passed in visits to friends, tours in Wales, Wharfedale, and the Lake District with Anne Lister, senior, a trip to Paris with Anne's father and sister, and, in 1824-1825, a long visit to Paris where Anne studied French under Countess Galvani whose husband was the discoverer of galvanism.

The photographs of Shibden Hall, on page 22, give an idea of this beautiful example of early fifteenth century architecture. The exact date of building is not known, but the deeds at Shibden Hall date back to 1420. The original timber building was added to in the seventeenth century, altered in the eighteenth, and added to again in the nineteenth century during Anne Lister's ownership, but the original is still clearly to be seen, and is the core of the whole building. The fifteenth century house consisted of a passage running from the south porch to the north door at the back, with the house body on the west and two parlours in the gable beyond, and a kitchen and buttery in the gable at the east end. Over these five rooms were five bedrooms.[5]

In the seventeenth century a buttery was built on the north side; the old buttery became a parlour and two rooms were added onto the east gable. This was the house as lived in by Anne Lister and it was not until after her uncle and aunt's death that she began the additions to the building. In 1838 she built a Norman tower at the west end, at the top of which was a room to be used as a library. In place of the upper kitchen and shop she built more extensive servants' quarters. A new and more elaborate staircase was made, and the ceiling of the house-body

---

[5] See *A short history of Shibden Hall* by T.W. Hanson: and also Halifax Antiquarian Society Transactions, 1907, 1910, 1915-17, 1921, 1925, and 1926 for a history of Shibden Hall (up to 1678), by John Lister.

was removed, thus making a lofty room, open to the roof. Shibden Hall remains like this today and, since the death of John Lister, in 1933, has been scheduled as a national monument and thrown open to the public as the Yorkshire Folk Museum. In 1923 it was purchased by a friend of John Lister's, Mr A.S. McCrea of Warley, and presented to the town after Mr Lister's death.

The part of Shibden Valley in which the Hall is situated is still unspoilt. One would not think that a hundred and fifty years ago it was a busy mining district. The land around Shibden Hall is undermined with disused coal-pits, and there are quarries and clay-pits in the neighbourhood.

The lake in the park was constructed in Anne Lister's lifetime, so that the water power could be used to work the mining machinery. There are coal-mining documents (bonds, leases, account books, etc) relating to the Shibden estate, dating from 1629-1895 now in the Calderdale archives. The mines and quarries were Anne Lister's chief source of income, thus when, towards the end of the nineteenth century, the output of coal was exhausted, her successors were dependent on the farm and cottage rents. These were insufficient, and consequently, in the present century, the sale of farms and land began, until only the old Hall and its grounds were left to the last of the Lister family.

As soon as all the business matters were settled, after James Lister's death in 1826, the two Miss Listers left Halifax for eighteen months' residence in Paris, mainly for the sake of the aunt's health. During this visit Anne made an extensive tour of Switzerland and Italy which is interestingly described in her letters. Travel was Anne's life-blood — 'I shall be like a bird escaped from its cage, when I am once again *en voyage*' she wrote to a friend.

The last twelve years of Anne's life were made up mainly of travel — to Switzerland in 1828, France, Belgium and Germany in 1829, the Pyrenees in 1830, with periods of study at the Sorbonne and Collège de France. In 1831 Miss Lister visited Holland, in 1833 Denmark, and in 1834 she paid a second visit to Switzerland. The Pyrenees were explored for a second time in 1838, and in 1839 the journey to the Caucasus, which was to cost Anne her life, was begun. The route lay through Belgium, Holland, Denmark, Sweden and Finland to Russia. The adventures and experiences are admirably described in the detailed letters.

It is not necessary here to described Anne Lister's personality, as her energy of character, seriousness of thought, and philosophy of life are so well revealed in her letters.

Anne Lister's sometimes idiosyncratic spelling and punctuation have been retained.

1

GEORGIAN GIRLHOOD

1800-1803

The letters written by Anne Lister in her childhood show a remarkable maturity of thought. The first letter, however, (written at the age of nine) is only noteworthy as an example of the type of letter written by dutiful children at the beginning of the last century. It is addressed to her Aunt, Anne Lister, at Shibden Hall, Halifax, and runs as follows:-

Dear Aunt

I beg pardon for not writing to you sooner my Mother intended sending my Improvement by my Father but she forgot I spent very pleasant Holidays at Christmas I hope this Letter will find you and all my Friends in good Health as I am at present. I like Music better then (sic) Dancing and am very happy at School I hope my Mother was better the last time you saw her my Grandmother is now at Bath.

Be so good as to give my Duty to my Uncles and Aunts and respects to inquiring Friends.

I am Honrd Aunt your
Dutiful Niece
Ann Lister

Ripon May 5 1800

An 'improvement' appears to be a sheet from a copy-book

showing a pupil's handwriting at a certain date. Among Anne Lister's letters is her 'Christmas Improvement' for 1801; it consists of carefully written copies of *Mind your words*, *Command your pen* and *Every moment of time is a moment of mercy*, in the usual copy-book style.

The next letter in the collection is remarkable for a child of twelve; it is written from Skelfler House, near Market Weighton, in the East Riding of Yorkshire, in a very regular hand and is addressed to the same aunt, who was then staying in Petergate, York.

Skelfleur Thursday February 3 1803

My dear Aunt

I am now going to write you a very long letter, and have to thank you for the Drawing Book you sent me, the Copys I think very pretty and well adapted to my young genious, I have begun of the first, but have not quite finished it. Marian was highly pleased with her present, she says you are a very good Aunt; you may be sure we were both very happy to hear from my Mother so good an account of your Health; she and my Father are gone this Afternoon to drink tea in Weighton, and in their absence I shall employ my time in writing to you I dont know what sort of a Letter I shall make of it, as I intend it to be a long one, and my Mother has particularly desired me say nothing upon my favourite subject of Farming, she says as we are going to leave Skelfleur we should turn our thoughts another way, perhaps I cannot do better than tell you some little of what I have been reading lately, for you know I was always fond of Books, my library is one of my greatest pleasures after a good ramble in the Fields I assure you I am very much pleased with the Georgical Essays,[1] I have read a little of the first and third Volumes, they are sure to be interesting to me throughout, for they are very improving and at the same time entertaining I was always fond of Farming and think I have a little taste that way; without Agriculture neither Commerce Arts or Sciences could flourish the Nation would not be so rich as it is, and we never could have carried on so long a war[2] as this last has been without it; Agriculture has several times been neglected and as many times encouraged, the different States finding the advantage of it there have been many Publications on the Subject it surely is now come to a very flourishing state, and no doubt will like every thing else go on improving. The Grecian history has pleased me much you know Mr Trant made me a present of the Roman History, what a brave people the Greeks in general were, and particularly the Spartans and Athenians to be sure they had some very great Generals, which gave them advantage over superior numbers, indeed I wonder that the Romans should have conquered them; what a dreadful retreat that must have been of Artaxerxes from the Hellespont Lysander a Spartan was a great General, he blocked up the Port of Aegos Potamos and took the whole Athenian Fleet excepting twelve Gallies which Conon contrived to escape with. Philip King of Macedon was a very great Man, he was very ambitious and gained many Battles. As my Letter draws to a conclusion, I must now make my request to you, which is, that when an opportunity offers and you have *leisure time*, you will have the goodness to purchase for me a Dictionary I mean one of the very best (pub)lications, one that will not only instruct me in Spelling but in the (proper?) and fashionable way of pronunciation. I have five Guineas to spare and I dont know how I can expend it better to my own satisfaction, then by a thing of that kind that will always be of use to me, when you have made the purchase, or let me know the sum you think it will be, I will remit you the Money, it will be a valuable addition to my collection of Books. My Father Mother and Marian unite with me in affectionate remembrance to you, and beg you will present their Compliments to Doctor and Mrs Hunter. Believe me my dear Aunt very sincerely Anne Lister.

Your Niece has just finished her Letter, the greatest part of which was wrote last night, it is entirely her own, I really cou'd not forbear smiling when she shew'd it me — but for your Brother I think I shou'd scarcely have let her send it — it seems out of character for such a giddy Girl — but you know she is a

---

[1] *Georgical Essays* by A. Hunter. 1803.

[2] The war with France, 1793-1802.

little high flown at times. On Sunday next she is to play the Organ, it is certainly a charitable act, as the young Man is under a penalty of forty pounds unless he procures some body to play for him in his absence, which would be an expensive but a very difficult matter to do. Anne has wrote her Letter sadly too small — but she has not forgot how to write large hand exceeding well. — adieu. — (Rebecca Lister)[3]

The next two letters were written by Anne when on a visit to her relations at Shibden Hall.

My dear Mother,

I am happy to inform you that we arrived safe at Halifax at seven o'clock on Monday night without any thing particular occuring we was in York at seven and were drove very well all the way I slept at Shibden Hall all night and was not much tired with my journey but was as you may suppose glad to get to Bed I called upon Mr Trant at Leeds but he was not at home I saw his Father who said he was not well that he was gone into the country for a little fresh air and that he did not expect him there soon he sent his compliments to you and my Father and hoped the Family was all well. My Uncle has begun harvest and has got part of a Field of Oats shorn he is at present very busy having a many things to do as soon as he possibly can My Uncle Joseph drank Tea with us last night he looked very ill and said that he had also begun and got a good deal cut indeed there was a great part of the Corn led as we came. Mr Midgley I daresay has got pretty nearly half of his stacked there has been very fine weather so far does Sam drive the Waggon yet I hope he and John say their lessons every Morning and that they begin to improve in their reading. The garden is well stocked with Fruit but Thieves have as is usual been at the apples once or twice there is a board ready to be put up to tell people that there are Man Traps in the Ground. Tell my Father we shall all be very glad to see him and I hope when he does come he intends to make a long stay. I will write to you again soon and then if I

---

[3] Postscript by Anne's mother, Rebecca Lister.

should want anything will let you know excuse this short letter for my Aunt is waiting of me to go to Halifax be so good as to give my Love to my Father Brothers and Sister and believe me to be your affectionate Daughter A Lister

PS. If there are any mistakes, pray excuse them for I have not time to correct them tell John Anderson and all my old Friends, not forgetting Mrs Dean that I have not forgot them give *John Anderson* sometimes if you please a little Beer in my name and take care of my things.

Shibden Hall August 30 1803.

My Uncle and aunts desire to be remembered to you all.

Shibden Hall Wednesday September 15 1803.

My dear Mother

I am happy to tell you that my Father arrived[4] ... safe on Monday Night after I was gone to Bed, I was very (mu)ch surprised to see him in the Morning not expecting (hi)m, till Evening, I received your Letter and was glad to (hear) that you were all well. You told me that Mr Trant had (got) married which I was very much astonished to hear, he (and) his Bride may very likely pay you a visit. I was glad (to hear?) that Mrs Midgley had got a little Boy, I hope she is ... well, pray when you see her give my best respects to her (and) Mr Midgley, by the next time you write they will have (a)ll their harvest in, tell Mrs Midgley she will be the first, I shall (go to?) see after I get Home. I should like to have a ride on the ... sometimes, as I believe I shall never ride anything else ... have not now time to write you a long Letter, you will think I am always in a hurry but indeed I think I do nothing but visit, Sunday I dined with Miss Mellins, Monday I went to see Mrs Nicholls, yesterday I dined at Mr Stopford's,[5] and today I am to drink Tea at Mr Greenwoods of Southowram, we dine at half past one, and shall set off directly after dinner. I am going to learn to sing with Mr Stopford, he will teach me in the public stile, I am to have two Lessons a Week. How I am dressed on a Sunday, I have got a new Bonnet, a new White Tippet, a pair of new Stays, and my new Frock made up. My Aunt desires me to thank you

31

for her Letter, which she is much obliged to you for, but will not answer it immediately as I am so good a correspondent, We were very much oblighed to you for the Game you sent us, which we received on Monday Morning, we had the Partridges to dinner yesterday which were very fine ones. Have you heard of Captain Akeds death, he died on the 8th of this Month at Dublin, Mrs Lister is going into mourning for him. Be so good when you write again as to tell me what sort of Lace my Aunt is to get for my best Frock, whet(her) it is to be Valencene or any other sort. You have sent me th(ree) double Muslin Handkerchiefs, I can very well spare you on(e) then I shall have two and they will be quite sufficient for (me?). I have got one of your single Muslin Handkerchiefs which (I will?) send you by my Father, as I can do very well without it.

Frills will all do very well. Mr Lee's son is going to begin (busi)ness on Monday. I am sorry I had not time to finish this L(etter) yesterday, but I hope you will excuse me saying any mo(re). The Miss Watkinsons and Miss Hannah Hudson are to dine (here?) today, and I have it to take to the Post Office. Miss Han(nah) Hudson along with her Sister, and Mr and Mrs G. Alex(ander) are to drink Tea here this afternoon. I dont know whether my Uncle and Aunt will be here or no. I shall write to Sam (on?) Saturday and Sunday and soon after then I will write to you again, and then it shall be a long Letter. My Father Uncles and Aunts desire to be remembered to you all, I beg you will give my Love to my Brothers and Sister. I hope you will write soon. I remain dear Mother your affectionate Daughter.

Anne Lister

Thursday Morning September 15 1803.

---

[4] Margin of letter torn away.

[5] Thomas Stopford, organist at Halifax Parish Church from 1766-1819.

2

ONE FRIEND TO ANOTHER

Anne left the Manor School, York, in 1806 while her West Indian friend, Eliza Raine, remained there for another year. A sentimental exchange of letters began and continued until 1814. Over eighty of Eliza's letters have been preserved, the melancholy nature of which seems to have been the precursor of her derangement: she was declared incurably insane in 1814. The letters, full of avowals of friendship, are interesting mainly in the light they throw on the life and character of Anne, and on the history and fashions of the day. A few extracts will suffice. The first letter, probably written in October 1806, is from Anne to Eliza who has just returned to school after spending the summer holidays with the Lister family.

My dearest Eliza,

So anxious am I to know whether you are comfortable and how you arrived at the Manor that I can scarcely persuade myself to have patience to wait a day or two for your ever welcome Epistle which though a poor substitute for your Company will give unspeakable pleasure to me whose only study is your happiness. I hope, my dear Girl, you are sufficiently a Philosopher to make you content in all stations and to consider every thing for the best and our parting as a circumstance prae-ordained for our future and greater comfort. Ah! dear Liz I'm preaching up Doctrine that is of little service to me as distracted to lose you I sigh and lament in vain, fully verifying the old

Proverb that the more you have the more you would have,

> (I study much to stay my greif (sic)
> and think on your letters for releif)(sic).

In a letter to Anne's mother, Mrs Jeremy Lister whom Eliza regarded as a mother, Eliza wrote (June 15 1807) 'York has been very hustling of late, the late Election[6] has given new brightness to the scene, and has afforded this ancient City a little more gaiety, than is usual; there has been great party spirit. Milton has proved victorious, they tell me Lascelles his opponent has made a firm determination never again to encounter so strong an antagonist for this City ... .'

---

[6] The June 1807 election was the first contested one for Yorkshire for sixty-six years. The poll opened on May 20 1807 and continued for fifteen days, during great excitement. Lord Milton was elected, with 188 more votes than Lord Lascelles.

3

BETWEEN BROTHER AND SISTER

1813

In 1813 Anne's favourite relative, her much loved younger brother Samuel, an Ensign in the 18th Foot, was stationed at Fermoy in County Cork. Anne's letters are full of sisterly advice to the brother on whom all her hopes were fixed for the revival of the family fortunes. She was to be sadly disappointed.

1, Laura Place, Bath. February 1813

I fear, my dear Sam, you have long thought me somewhat neglectful, to use no harsher term, in having allowed your last affectionate letter to remain so long unanswered & unnoticed . . . . Here then let me resume the thread of my story. My visit to L(angton) was protracted to the 1st of December, when Isabella, Charlotte, Miss Mariana Belcombe and myself filled Mr N(orcliffe)'s chaise, disembarked at his house in Petergate, and proclaimed the intended arrival of the rest of the family in the course of a day or two. The first night, much to the merriment of our party, we all crammed ourselves (in two beds tho') into the same room. Early the next morning the Norcliffes went to visit a friend near Beverley, and I set off to the Duffins where I had promised to stay till Isabella and I went to Halifax. Here I was rejoiced to find all well, and spent a fortnight as usual — that is — lounging away the mornings in calls &c — and the evenings in playing cards — on the 14th (Decr) my friend and I took the mail for Halifax, and got there about seven — finding all in bed, except three damsels who rushed out to hail our arrival. You knew from my last that Eliza was expecting to leave Halifax for a change of climate. She had had an auction, sold all her furniture, and was well settled at the Hot Wells near Bristol before my native hills beheld again the beauty of my visage. This circumst(ance) ...[1]... arrived announcing Norcliffe's unexpected arrival in England which of course hastened my darling's[2] departure and she left us immediately. As I had for the last year been so very little at home, it was agreed I should only spend a week in York before our proceding Southwards. I therefore spent three weeks quietly at North Bridge, and on Monday February 1 again forsook my native hills, and supped in Petergate. Here I was delighted to find Norcliffe a good natured, sensible, agreeable young man, much better recovered from his wound than I expected, and the rest of my friends in high health and spirits. Among the rest I had no small pleasure in seeing again Miss M. Belcombe. But who is *she*, perhaps you'll say? She is Isabella's most intimate friend, who came to us before we left Langton, and made the last fortnight of our stay there doubly interesting. She is indeed a charming girl, and, from the real worth of her character, has gained no mean portion of my esteem and regard. After spending a most agreeable week in Petergate, on Tuesday morning February 9 — about half past nine, Mr N(orcliffe)'s coach and four, and chaise and pair carried off our whole party, and surely we had one of the loveliest days that ever beamed in the same season of the year. We reached Sheffield in good time, and here we slept the first night. In the morning we reconnoitre'd the town and were much interested with being shewn over one of the largest plate manufactories. We then pursued our journey, and took up our night's quarters at the King's Arms (I think it was) in Derby. Here we saw the best porcelain manufactory, and were led from room to room to see every process of it. There is also a very large silk manufactory close upon the river (Derwent) but this we had not time to explore. It is really a nice neat city, and surrounding country very pretty. From this we went forward to Birmingham where we slept. Here we saw the whole routine of pin making, and, thro' a letter of introduction from Mrs Staunton were shewn over the whole of Mr Tomason's extensive works. Here we saw again the process of plating. Saw the mode of gem cutting and setting, and artificial gem making — the manufacture of cutlery, of striking medals, stamping, and milling provincial tokens, of livery buttons, of glass cutting,

& papier maché of which tea trays and such things are made. With our heads full of the wonders we had seen, we journeyed onwards to Worcester where we spent the fourth night of our travels. This is an uncommonly pretty city. Here we looked over Chamberlains beautiful collection of the Worcester china. In point of taste of design, this I think exceeds the Derby — which, tho' at first a better white, is said to lose this perfection by time, and turn rather more yellowish. They do not however attempt at Worcester the elegant biscuit work in which they so much excel at Derby — biscuit work is the name for a sort of entirely white porcelain of which they form various beautiful ornaments, as vases singly, figures and groups. Of course we went to the Cathedral. Nothing struck me so much as the fine monument of Bishop Hough by Roubillac — the Bishop is represented on a bed dying and a (?) of religion supporting him. Hence we got to Rodborough fifteen miles from Bath, where after . . .³ many people at that at Halifax. I will not however run much farther into descriptions, as the briefest account of Bath would exceed the limits of my paper. I shall only say it is a delightful place abounds in every species of agreeable amusement and forms the most striking contrast imaginable to the neighbouring city of Bristol — the one most beautiful, the other the ugliest city in England. The former abounds in fine buildings, the latter has hardly a good street in it. On Saturday the 20th, at nine in the morning, Isabella and I set off in one of the coaches for the Hot Well where Eliza is, about a mile as I think I have before told you, from Bristol. We found her in good spirits, nearly recovered by the change of climate, and purposing to return to the north, and settle in York in about a month. She inquired after you very kindly and particularly, and desired me to give her best remembrances when I wrote. We staid with her till six in the evening of the following, and reached home a little after eight. The Hot Well is about half a mile from Clifton the loveliest village in England. The scenery would far exceed my powers of description, even if I had time and paper to sport with *ad libitum*. But I must now think of answering your letter and speaking more particularly of myself. Let me then say no more of Bath, than that I am, and have every reason to be, as happy here as my dear Sam's most sanguine wishes can desire and am as well too as I ever was in my . . .⁴. I must however confess my first anxiety is to hear from you. If you write but a few lines

37

it will satisfy me as I shall feel well assured you would do more if it were in your power. My suspense about you is really wretched — as yet I am quite uncertain where you are, or where you may be. Half a line to tell me this and that you are well will make me easy. Now I hardly know what to think unless it be that uncertainty about our friends is of all things the least comfortable. I am glad however to see from the Army list just come out for this month that you have three Ensigns below you.

Friday morning — 12th March 1813 — You will wonder, my dear Sam, as well you may to see the former part of my letter dated last month. The truth is I have had it by me these three weeks; being so unwilling, whilst uncertain where you are, to send my pages hunting after at nobody knows what expense, that I was determined to wait any time for a frank. I have at last got one and sincerely hope it will reach you soon and safely. Again let me entreat you to write to me immediately on receiving it. A few lines will satisfy if you have opportunity to send . . . [5] the army. I wish to God your plans were fixed. Do let me hear of them by some means. Remember, my dear Sam, because absent from you I am not the less, but more anxious about whatever concerns you. Your happiness will be a great step towards my own, but believe me, if I had all the good things this world can afford, all would be to little purpose without the assurance of your welfare, in which I shall ever take an equal, if not a more anxious interest, than in my own. You my dear dear Sam, are the last remaining hope and stay of an old, but lately drooping family. Sieze it in its fall. Renovate its languid energies; rear it with a tender hand, and let it once more bloom upon the spray. Ah! let the well-ascended blood that trickles in your veins stimulate the generous enthusiasm of your soul, and prove it is not degenerated from the spirit of yr ancestors.

---

[1] Part of the letter cut away here.

[2] ie. Isabella's departure.

[3] Letter cut away here.

[4] Letter cut away here.

'I feel the glow of patriot zeal'. But adieu — I can no more,

Sincerely & affectionately yrs A.L.

Poor fellow! He was drowned ab(ou)t three o'clock in ye afternoon of ye 19th of ye following month (June 1813) while bathing in ye river Blackwater, near Fermoy, County of Cork, Ireland. This mem(orandu)m written by his affectionate and afflicted A.L.

---

[5]Part cut away. An undated fragment.

4

PARIS IN THE EARLY NINETEENTH CENTURY

1819

In May 1819 Miss Lister and her aunt set off on a sight-seeing visit to Paris, where they stayed for seventeen and a half days. The only correspondence relating to this visit is a copy of a long letter (seventy-one quarto sheets) to Mr and Mrs Duffin, which Miss Lister wrote on her return home. There are many impressions of foreign travel and sight-seeing in existence, but this account is worthy of reproduction in part as being that of a thoughtful and intelligent woman of the early nineteenth century. That Mr Duffin valued it highly is clear from his reply:-
... 'I have read only a few pages of your tour, it is too precious to devour all at once, I am delighted with it and shall preserve it as a Guide should I ever visit Paris ... .'

My dear Mr and Mrs Duffin,

I dare not guess what you will say on seeing a thing which must at first, perhaps at last, appear much more like a tiresome journey-book, than a letter. The fact is, I had just finished my epistle in, I should be ashamed to say how many foolscap sheets, when my uncle and aunt laid it under embargo, and determined to make me pay a transit duty of a complete copy of the whole. It occurred to me it would be better to have the sheets stitched than send them loose, and to confine myself to one quire of letter-paper as a limit which it would be unreasonable on your account, and imprudent on my own, to transgress: this will oblige me to leave out much which, however amusing to us at the time, has yet so little novelty and interest beyond the moment and

40

the very individuals concerned, that I should scarce have patience to write it a second time.

A journey to London, before the days of Palmer[1] and mail-coaches, was a serious undertaking; and people were as careful to make their wills, before they set off, as they would now be to provide themselves with philosophical instruments to measure an arc of the meridian, or the heights of the Andes. A journey to Paris was of some moment to those whose step had scarcely wandered from their native home; yet how insignificant when compared with the general round of continental travel! On a second reading of my pages, I should have buried them for ever in my writing-desk; but I had said I would write, and, if we cannot please ourselves, it is always, perhaps, incumbent on us to shew that we would willingly attempt to please others: yet I thought of you so often, perhaps, as you would scarcely believe, considering the many things which necessarily occupy the attention of manager-general in a five weeks' excursion.[2] I longed to surprise you by a Paris Post-mark, and not least among the pleasures I anticipated was that of affording you a few pages of entertainment, or, at least, of proving to you, my dear Mr Duffin, that novelty of scene, however striking, cannot banish from my remembrance how much I owe to you the power of enjoying them by the preservation of a life which shall have eked out its little span in this world, ere I can forget or cease to offer, with heart-felt satisfaction the small but grateful and affectionate tribute of my lasting thanks.

As nothing particular happened to us on the road, I shall omit the eight or ten pages giving an account of our life and adventures during our six days' journey, and merely say that we fortunately determined, on our arrival at Calais, to proceed in the last and newly established post-coach — that we everywhere met with the utmost civility and attention — went on our way very pleasantly and very comfortably, and dined at our hotel in Paris (Hôtel des Ambassadeurs, rue Ste Anne)

---

[1] John Palmer, 1742-1818, projector of mail coaches (1784).

[2] They were away for twenty-five days, seventeen and a half of which were spent in Paris.

at five o'clock in the afternoon of Saturday May 15. We had observed few gentlemen's seats along the road — met very few carriages or people, and, as we came in sight of the far-famed city, could not help exclaiming, How unlike the bustling scene about London! We thought the entrance through the barrier of St Denis shabby. A channel down the middle of narrow streets — rough bowlder stone pavements with no causeways, and high, untidy, comfortless looking houses struck us forcibly, after the so opposite appearance of our own capital. However, we found our Hotel, to which we had been strongly recommended, quite what we wished (among its numerous inhabitants only two English besides ourselves). Madame Joly provided us a good dinner — we engaged the *valet de place* who had served Mrs Best and her sister — we were in a few hours as much settled as if we had been there for months, and our only anxiety was to make the best use of our time and see everything, or at least, out of such an abundance of objects worthy of attention and, as we soon learnt to acknowledge, of admiration, to select those of most general notoriety and importance.

Regarding the sights, Anne Lister found the Louvre even more magnificent than any description she had heard of or read. The Tuileries Palace had an air of princely magnificence where, on her second visit Anne 'had a full view of Monsieur, the Duke and Duchess d'Angoulême and the Duke de Berri ... The Duchess wore a lilac silk pelisse trimmed and flounced with blonde: her appearance was peculiarly interesting, and, though perhaps without the majestic dignity of some of our own royal family, yet she looked a princess not unworthy the oldest Kingly race in Europe. The royal dukes wore quite plain, dark-coloured uniforms; but the attendant marshals were covered with gold embroidery'.

She was disappointed in the Tuileries Gardens — 'not a blade of grass to be seen, but one dull carpet of gravel studded with benches and common straw-bottomed kitchen-chairs piled on one another in every direction, or already occupied by the countless and motley multitudes that thus while away more particularly the evening hours. All this was a scene very little resembling English gardens, or the delightful rurality of English grounds. It was here, however, that we felt ourselves most peculiarly in Paris — that we soon learnt to sit or saunter like

42

the rest — to enjoy the verdant canopy that shaded off the blinding glare of the sun, and to pay our two sols apiece for chairs, and the like sum per paper for half an hour or an hour's reading of the *Moniteur*, or other journals of the day. It amused us to skim over the regular notices of fêtes religious and profane, theatricals, and, above all, English parliamentary debates, as quoted from our newspapers, stating the ruined treasury, the insupportable taxation, the disturbed population of England, contrasting with flourishing finance, the easy burdens, the prosperous tranquillity of France.'

Other places the two Miss Listers visited included La Place du Carrousel, the bridges of Paris ('not to be compared with those in London'), the floating baths consisting 'of a double row of two stories of small rooms, or closets, very neatly ornamented, and altogether containing 140 sufficiently large bathing-tubs: the awning, stretched from the roof of these rooms over each side of the vessel, forms a pretty covered walk shaded with pots of orange-trees, myrtles, etc.: there are communications by flights of wooden stairs descending from the bridge, and the whole seems very well managed. At a little distance are inferior floating-baths, for the lower classes (*les ouvriers*) at four or six sols a bath. During the heat of a Parisian summer, we could imagine nothing more wholesome or agreeable than bathing: and, in this respect, the city seems amply provided with every convenience. The floating-baths are not, probably, frequented by nobility; but the bains Chinois on the Italian boulevard, and those de Tivoli on the Chaussée d'Antin, as, I daresay, many others, are furnished with every comfort and luxury.

'Not far from the floating-baths, and in other places, scattered over the river, our attention used to be caught by the washing vessels in which the washerwomen beat away with their flat sticks, and kept up a din almost like that of don Quixotte's fulling mills. The village, or town of St Cloud, is a very favourite place, where they are perpetually at work all along the river-side; however, the specimen we had by no means answered our expectation: our things were exceedingly stiffened, and scented with a smell we did not like, and though my aunt word black, cost at the rate of twelve or fourteen francs a week. To us, also, who had been accustomed to see charcoal as a sort of rarity, used only for special purposes, the countless barges full of it, were an object of novelty, and, together with the large and beautifully piled fire-wood stacks, instantly reminded us why the atmosphere incumbent over Paris was almost perfectly clear, while that over our own capital might have served Homer to represent the smoke of Vulcan's forge.'

At the Conservatoire des Arts et Métiers the English ladies 'lamented we had not some parallel institution in London' though they found nothing 'in this great national collection of machinery and all sorts of instruments and specimens of workmanship ... superior, whilst most things appeared decidedly inferior to what we had at home. You would have smiled at some of the models of ploughs still in common use, and at thrashing-machines, where the utmost effort of art was to set in motion a few flails.'

The Gobelins tapestry was 'more beautiful than we could have imagined'. They enjoyed visits to the Mint, la Musée des Mines, la Bibliothèque du Roi, and the Institut Library where they met the Greek scholar and patriot, Adamantios Coraes (1748-1833).

Le Jardin des Plantes was especially interesting to the naturalists — the menagerie — the botanic gardens — the Museum of Natural History and Cabinet of comparative anatomy, presided over by M. Cuvier whom they hoped to meet at a later date.

Among the eleven churches they visited were the beautiful Ste Geneviève where 'On entering the vaults we were at once struck by the tombs of Voltaire and Rousseau; that of the latter having at one end a door a little open from which projected a hand holding a lighted torch close to a terrestrial globe, seemed one of those pretty ideas for which the French are so famed', and St Denis where they witnessed the annual ceremony of the recovery of the bones of St Denis, St Rustic, and St Eleutère, attended by the Cardinal Prince Talleyrand and numerous high ranking clergy.

The two Yorkshirewomen were such avid sightseers that they 'had only time for two meals a day; breakfast at nine — dinner at five, six or seven. The bread was good, from our rolls almost three quarters of a yard long, to small thin loaves (such as are eaten by the lower classes) with a little rye in them. The butter always fresh and excellent — the café au lait very good; the potages, the rôtis, the bouillis, the divers &cs à la sauce piquante, the desserts — all were good; we liked everything but what they called au naturel, and cabbage.

'The wines, too, and water were good: of the former we had about as many varieties as dinners. Burgundy from 1s. to 3s.6d. a bottle, Bordeaux at about 4s. Grave, Soterne, and several others at 3s.4d., Champagne (or in English Champaign), both sorts and excellent, 5s.5d., our favourite Hermitage, from the famous vineyards of Tournon on the Rhone, at 4s.2d. Many English people are ill in Paris; the Seine water is said to disagree with them. I drank it both at Breakfast and dinner; it was clear and palatable: my aunt, too, drank it at dinner, and neither of us ever felt better in our lives, than during the seventeen days and a half of our stay in Paris. We lived entirely à la Français, and not a pain, nor an ache warned us to desist. To our two meals we allotted about two hours a day, and, with this exception, every moment, more than once from six in the morning to eleven at night, was occupied in seeing a great deal, and in observing and remembering as much as we could. You will smile, perhaps, at the motley order in which I go from one thing to another. I do assure you that, amid so hasty a survey of such a multiplicity of objects, the mental records of an experienced tourist, are naturally subject to a little confusion of arrangement that it would take more time to methodize, than I had any idea of six or eight months ago. To write at the time what you have seen today or yesterday, is one thing; it is another to sit down after your return home, not knowing where, or with what to begin. My mind with its crowd and jumble of ideas, is like a coffer full of ballots; I put my hand in, as it were, and chance alone determines which, and what sort of one, comes first: consider, then, the caprice of chance, and do not wonder that, after soups and wines are drawn cemeteries and catacombs.

'Of the former there are four principal ones, (instituted about the year 1800), at the four extremities of the city; that of Mont-Louis, where still stands the house of Louis the 14th's confessor, father Lachaise — of Montmartre, — of Ste Catherine, and of Mont-Parnasse; of these, as we had only time to visit one, we, of course, chose Mt Louis, confessed the first in extent, situation, and the beauty of its monuments which are generally in good style, and classic taste. We were present at a funeral. A neat herse, drawn by two horses, stopped at the gate; and, after a short delay at the place (salle de deuil) where they stop to arrange the bearers, etc., the corpse, covered with a neat black pall, preceded by a priest and a police-officer in the royal livery (dark blue and silver lace), was brought to the sloping edge of the great square pit; the priest muttered a few words. The taking off the pall discovered a rough unplaned deal box, and the officer saw it let down, and placed close by three others which we could distinguish through the thin sprinkling of sand. The only mourner, a well-dressed middle-aged man, cast one long look behind at the last farewell to his daughter, and quietly walked off alone. Another corpse was waiting to be placed alongside the last; but we did not stay to witness the same ceremony over again. The pit, they said, was quite new; and we had seen the fourth coffin laid on the lowmost tier which, at a random guess, might be gradually surmounted by eight or nine more, still leaving room for two or three feet of soil on the top of the last. If we mistook not, they told us a new pit was opened every year. Remember, it is only offered as a random guess; but, to the best of our recollection, it would not surprise us if the area of this fosse would hold six or seven rows of sixteen or twenty coffins each: they are merely boxes, not apparently of superfluous dimensions, and pushed quite close side by side. Suppose six rows of sixteen each to equal one tier; then one tier would contain ninety-six coffins, and, if the pile should be only seven tiers high, $96 \times 7 = 672$, and thus one grave would swallow up in its dismal gorge near seven hundred bodies. But till late in the last century, when Paris had no other cemetery than that of the Innocents, from twelve to fifteen hundred were laid together in the common trenches. These pits, however, of modern days, are only at the foot of Mt Louis, and, as you ascend the hill, you get among the resting places of separate individuals, wattled round, or parted off with low trellis; a weeping willow or a cypress planted at the head — a little wooden cross beneath, and flowers or rose bushes blooming over the grave. From these, as you still advance, you in every sense of the word reach the higher regions of the dead; inscriptions first, then marble tombs and sculptured figures — shady walks and fragrant shrubs — while the eye ranges over the domes and palaces of Paris, or turns from the beautiful little Ionic temple of d'Urquino, to the Gothic chapel of Ney, or the stately marble obelisk that records the memory of Massena, and frowns over the blood-stained chateau of Vincennes. *Massena mort le Avril 4 1817*, is the only inscription, and a mantle of lillies encircling his coat-armour, attests in brief simplicity his loyalty to the house of Bourbon.'

Miss Lister gives particulars of the cost of different types of grave, from twenty-seven francs plus the cost of the monument and, in the common grave, one place among the seven hundred would cost sixteen francs. 'What an excellent comment on the absurdity and impracticability of "liberty and equality" in this world' she wrote!

After a visit to the catacombs, Anne remarked '. . . after half an hour's traversing these vallies of death, we were glad to bid them, as we hoped, a last farewell, and hastened to emerge into the realms of day'. And so on to the Luxembourg Gardens, the Observatory, Le Palais Bourbon, the kitchens of the Hotel des Invalides where meals for four thousand private officers were cooked.

In order to have plenty of time at Versailles, the two sightseers left their hotel soon after six a.m. for the two hours' drive: they particularly admired Le Petit Trianon. On the way back they visited the china manufactory at Sèvres. Anne describes some of the beautiful pieces there and gives their prices.

The Palace at St Cloud was considered 'worthy to have been the favourite residence of Buonaparte. It is still furnished according to his taste, and truly it was a taste not unworthy of an emperor'. The seventeen day visit continued without a let-up, from Vincennes, to Malmaison, St Germain, Tivoli (where Anne junior ventured on the exciting Montagne Russe), with visits to theatres but, wrote Anne 'As we were sometimes rather tired, and sometimes unable to get home in time, we saw less of the theatres than we wished'. They enjoyed the Ombres Chinoises — 'We were almost dissolved with heat, and the society was not the courtly circle of the Tuileries; but the performance began with an excellent fantocine representation of Henry the 4th, and his rescuing the fair Gabrielle from the enchanted forest was capital: the music is pretty, and the songs were sung very fairly: to this succeeded a pretty little exhibition of Chinese lights, and the whole was concluded with the shadows. Forty or fifty animals, birds and beasts, successively walked, ran, flew, or fed upon the stage so naturally, it would have been an excellent help to any lecture on zoology. A woodman cut down a row of trees, lastly mounted a ladder, fell down and broke his neck, and left his wife lamenting and consoling herself: the finishing scene was between a physician and his patient. We, as well as everyone else, laughed exceedingly, and could not help acknowledging that this real Chinese invention was an amusement, "which one can hardly see the first time without pleasure". It seems to have been first imitated in Europe by the Italians at Bologna. The principle is curious enough: it consists in moving, by pegs fastened to them, small figures cut of pasteboard, the joints of which are all pliable, behind a piece of fine painted gauze placed before an opening in a curtain, in such a manner as to exhibit various scenes, according to pleasure; while the opening, covered with gauze, is illuminated towards the apartment where the spectators sit, by means of light reflected from a mirror; so that the shadows of the pegs are concealed. When it is requisite to cause a figure to perform a variety of movements, it is necessary to have several persons, who must be exceedingly expert. When a snake is to be represented gliding, the figure, which consists of delicate rings, must be directed, at least, by three assistants. In fact, the amusement does credit to Chinese ingenuity — it was very well managed, and we were exceedingly entertained.'

In this account of a visit to Paris in 1819, Anne describes the excellent cafés and their frequenters. 'These cafés (Le Palais Royal and Le Café des Milles Colonnes), the first in Paris, and certainly elegant resorts of luxury, together with the gambling rooms and bagnios, are above the shops: in the cellars beneath them are inferior restaurateurs, and cafés, and places of amusement frequented by the lower orders of society. The Café des Aveugles, so called from its band of blind musicians, is a famous rendez-vous of motley conversation and intrigue. In the topmost story, the windows of which are in the roof, are collected the most lost and profligate characters of both sexes, and here may be seen the very last extremity of vice: there is, however, as it has been just remarked, an excellent police — soldiers everywhere on guard to prevent the whispers of disturbance, and there need be no hesitation to assert that any well-disposed person may walk the galleries of the Palais Royal, or any street in Paris, with as much security, at midnight, as beneath the broad meridian of noon. 'Tis true some of the histories of the Palais Royal shock decorum, and all common sense: from the salons where the Duke de Montmorenci and many of the nobility waste their fortunes at the gambling table, to the chambers for which it may be more intolerable than for some far-famed cities of the olden times, there may be — doubtless there is — a sad

"Abomination of desolation"; but a thick veil covers the exterior of deformity — it does not meet you barefaced as in the streets and theatres of London, and, whatever you may read, or hear of from your friends, you cannot really know these things without seeking after them, nor see them without being shut within the doors.'

The two ladies concluded that the Parisians did not live much at home, judging by the crowded cafés. Their landlady, Madame Joli, described how she lived:- 'Madame, contrary to the early hours of Paris, breakfasted at ten — had their accounts to settle and taxes to pay (she said they were always coming to her for something or other); but had a great many friends. Always went out in an afternoon, and, like the rest of this out-of-doors-living people, was never guilty of being at home when she had nothing particular to do. Hence we accounted for the crowds that were sitting, walking, talking, reading, sewing, and in the public gardens and on the boulevards — the full theatres, and other places of amusement, for they have their Sadler's Wells, Olympics, &c., &c., the bustling cafés, and all the stir of busy entertainment.'

Regarding popular feeling, Anne Lister wrote: 'We never discovered any warmth of loyalty to the Bourbons. Our valet was a loyalist, and he said there were a great many; but that there were, also, many who liked the Emperor because he gave them fêtes — all the workmen liked him because he gave them plenty of employment, and all the army because he was a hero, and led them to glory. Madame Joli, our maîtresse d'hôtel, and the widow of an officer tolerably high in Napoleon's commissariat, would talk, and, in a whisper, and with a most significant shrugging of the shoulders, amuse us exceedingly. "There were many English who loved the Emperor, and many who acknowledged that we had no right to choose them a ruler. Everybody doted on those brave men who were the friends of Lavalette, and they had been cheered wherever they went. Napoleon lived in the hearts of those who loved the glory of their country, and numbers always wore his picture. The sale of it was prohibited, but she could get it for us if we chose". She took us one day into her lodging room, and shewed us three beautiful miniatures of the two Napoleons, and Maria Louisa. "It is our only hope", said she, "that the Bourbons will leave no legitimate children, and then we shall have the son of our

Emperor — in fact, it was our prince regent who now ruled at the Tuileries". She told us the King was a very good man, and, as a man, everyone liked him; but he was not fit for their King. *"Voila,"* she said, pointing upwards, *"l'empereur — Eléphant; le roi"*, pointing to the floor, — *"mouche"*. It was one of her tenets, that there is a great and good god whom we ought to thank for all his blessings; but he does not command us — he would not be pleased to see us — do nothing else but thank him; *"mais le roi, il prit toujours, toujours, toujours"*. This was, likewise, urged of the duchess d'Angoulême; and the address the French clergy have lately presented to the Pope, lamenting the low estate of religious consideration towards them, might not, perhaps, be exaggerated or unjust. But this is a gainsaying age; the Parisians smile at pomps and processions which their forefathers would have venerated — estimate relics, perhaps, as they do the skulls at the catacombs, according to the beauty of their arrangement — and shrug their shoulders at *"les superstitions des prêtres"*. The Duke d'Angoulême had lately made himself more popular by visiting the different public charities; and other institutions; but we heard nothing of Monsieur, and nothing *for* the Duke de Berri. "I might have still kept my rank and emoluments", said M. Guillieu, "changing only the name of my service from imperial to royal, as many of my friends have done; but I would not receive the pay of a sovreign *'qui je n'aime pas'*. All this, however, was under the roof of our own apartments in our own hotel; for in public — in the gardens reading the papers — on the boulevards — at the restaurateurs and cafés — we never heard conversation turn on any offensive political subject. We occasionally saw foolish, trumped up stories about Buonaparte; but the French press is, doubtless, quite under the control of 'the powers that be', and one could not, perhaps, as in England, tell a man's politics from his newspaper".'

Spare time was sometimes spent strolling along the boulevards where 'The book-stalls, the prints, the fiddles and flutes, the people, the carriages — all had a novelty of grouping that diverted us exceedingly — all around was a scene of gaiety and cheerfulness; yet, we must again declare, our eye never glanced upon an unbecoming familiarity, nor did we once overhear a word which we understood to be improper. The boulevards are, in short, so striking, they must be mentioned by everyone, and admired by most'.

As for the roads in Paris, Anne Lister considered there was much less traffic than in London or even Halifax. 'Tho' we walked about as much as possible, we were not much incommoded, even in the most public streets, by carriages of any description: there seemed to us very little stir of the wheel kind at any time, and the utmost we saw was nothing to Northgate in Halifax on a busy market-day. How, or when, the inhabitants supplied their magazines of stores that required carting, we could not make out, as a cart or waggon so rarely appeared, we surely did not see above half a dozen the whole seventeen days and a half; and, what struck us as more extraordinary, we only passed three or four the whole way from Calais to Paris, not one in any of our excursions afterwards thence into the country, and not one, absolutely not one, the whole way from Paris to Dieppe: of the carriages, in going we passed one coach, our rival from Calais, and close to Paris, between three and four in the afternoon, counted two or three cabriolets: in returning we met one solitary cabriolet, whose gentleman driver, forgetting both his fair companion and the reins of his horse to stare at my *petit chapeau*, the animal stumbled, and down they came altogether. They may well have no turnpikes, and government may afford to keep the roads in repair; for if they are never more travelled than they were when we saw them, they may last, without the breaking of a single flint on them, from generation to generation. We happened, too, to pass through Beauvais on a market-day, and the grande place was full of stalls and people, a busy bustling scene: it is a very considerable town, chief of the department of the Oise. On a market-day at home we have repeatedly counted fourteen or fifteen carts passing the bridge at once; yet saw we nothing all along the road save two or three women, in their white lapetted caps, white jackets, and coloured petticoats, riding aside on huge wooden packsaddles, and as many men walking by the side, or at a distance. We certainly witnessed few signs of an overflowing population, and, surely it will be long ere Mr Malthus, famous doctor of political proportions (the geometrical progression of people to the arithmetrical progression of means of subsistence) need alarm the inhabitants of Artois, Picardy, the isle of France, or even the Gallic bread-and-cider-garden of Normandy . . . .

'Musing on what we had seen and heard, and with a sigh of regret as the domes and steeples of Paris were gradually lost to view, we commenced our journey homewards at half past five in the morning on Wednesday 2nd June, and, after a most agreeable route thro' Pontoise and Gisors, got to Rouen, a distance of near seventy-three miles, a little after seven in the evening, our rate of travelling, as we were two hours at Gisors, being full six miles an hour. As we passed St Denis (tho' little after six in the morning), we were struck with the early gaiety of a cotillon-set dancing away in high glee, that very gracefully, to the fiddle of one of the young men of the party. We lost sight of vines at Pontoise and entered on the cider-country. They were everywhere mowing the lucerne, and occasionally, we observed, a little clover: near Paris there was a little lucerne-hay housed, but the greater part seemed in large cock. About half way between Gisors and Rouen, rye began to give place to wheat, and we came to some of the best land in Normandy. M. Rosière is the chief landed proprietor in the neighbourhood in Ecouis (about twenty miles from Rouen), has his chateau at a little distance, and is a country squire of very high importance with an income of 150,000 francs (£6,250). It was near the very pretty village of Fleuri, where there is a large bleaching establishment, that the cabriolet was overturned on account of my little English hat. Everywhere in Normandy they seemed to use wheel-ploughs worked by one man and two horses. We passed several picturesque and beautiful villages, and, particularly as we approached Rouen, were strongly reminded of England. In many of the neat white cottages, embossed in orchard, we could have lived and almost grown romantic, tho' this, perhaps, was momentary illusion, for time had staid the feverish dream of youth.

'The first view of Rouen from Mount Catharine — a bold height about 380 feet above the Seine — is strikingly beautiful: at the foot of this semi-circular range of hill, which forms a commanding line of boundary, the river, broken by wooded islands, rolls majestically along; the city with its hundred thousand inhabitants covers an ample space, and a rich country is everywhere studded with hamlets and orchards. The quay was full of people, there was a good deal of shipping and an appearance of commercial interest and cheerfulness that well bespoke the prosperity of the town: it is by many degrees the oldest-looking place we ever saw, not exceeding Chester; the streets are very narrow — what they call the *grande* rue St Jean is not so wide as the narrowest part of Coney Street — and the houses being very high and the stories projecting, the eye has little to fear from intensity of light. The river seems about as broad as the Thames at Westminster, and its bridge of boats, well worth examination, can be taken in pieces in an hour, if danger be apprehended from floods or ice. We stood for some moments enchanted with the prospect: the sun was setting magnificently, and such scenery aided by the parting majesty of day, was peculiarly beautiful. Rouen, is indeed, interesting altogether — to the antiquary, the historian, and particularly the commercial economist, as being the Manchester of France. We were told the town had been much benefitted by the peace, and that the cotton-trade was very flourishing. Two or three large and handsome establishments, a mile or two lower down the river, had the air of chateaux rather than cotton-mills. After seeing the cathedral and making the best use of our time we could, we pursued our journey between ten and eleven the next morning (Thursday June 3), and reached Dieppe — a distance of thirty-four miles — a little after five.

'Of the four stages the first and last were far the prettiest; the valleys among the limestone downs in the neighbourhood of Dieppe were agreeably diversified with picturesque villages, and the town itself might almost pass for English. We had just time to take a little stroll along the grande Place and the principal street, and embarked on board the *Nautilus packet* at half past six. It was near an hour before we cleared the harbour, and we soon afterwards got rid of our pilot and custom house officer. The people watched us from the pier for a considerable time. I took my station at the stern, looking back upon the town and coast till distance and the shades of evening had almost shut them out of sight: the sun set gloriously, and a refreshing breeze just murmured along our canvas and curled the surface of the deep. We were about a dozen passengers. A fat French bourgeoise from Dieppe, going to London to see her son, sat on deck till nine, with only her white linen cap on her head, and not even a shawl over her shoulders: she kept up a constant clack to the amusement of a Miss Pelham and myself who had gradually witnessed the rest go off squeamish to bed: she, poor girl! was soon obliged to follow, for the breeze had freshened considerably, and I, having begged a berth in their open sociable, wrapt myself in a box-coat, and slept as soundly as ever in my life. Anxiety to see the sun rise, awoke me just in time: it was a glorious sight — I saw it to great advantage, and was indescribably gratified. My eyes were scarcely closed again, ere nature had replaced her seal of slumber, and I awoke no more till my aunt, seated on deck in wan and woful plight, and a long line of Albion's white cliffs burst full upon my view. We were all impatience to get on shore — the last two or three hours seemed tediously long — a boat came alongside us at ten, and at eleven we had landed on this favoured island, the admiration of every enlightened and impartial mind, and where the wise man sees abundant reason to be satisfied and happy.

'We left Brighton at three — got to town (fifty-three miles) in six hours, and, after seeing as much, perhaps, as it was possible to see of our own capital in five days and a half, reached Shibden in the evening of Saturday 12th June. Few, perhaps, of the motley multitude who have crossed the channel, have more enjoyed their excursion than my aunt and myself: we liked Paris exceedingly, and should be sorry to think we ''parted like Ajut — never to return''. Be this, however, as it may, *I* have had a double pleasure — that of visiting the place which of all others I most wished to see, and of dwelling thro' so many pages on the thought and remembrance of those friends whose early kindness will never lose its record in my heart, nor fail to be returned with warm and lasting gratitude by one who is always, my dear Mr and Mrs Duffin, very truly and affectionately yours. A. Lister.

Shibden Hall — Wednesday December 22 1819.'

This letter, which so ably describes post-revolutionary France, also shows Anne Lister's powers of minute observation; she had the true writer's gift of taking an interest in everything — whether it was the size of tombs or the clothes worn by the Duchesse d'Angoulême — and of concise description.

5

BY STEAM-PACKET AND POST CHAISE
TO PARIS

1822

White Horse, Leeds. Friday morning (quarter to Six).
30 August 1822.

I have quarter of an hour to spare, my dear aunt, and you shall have it; for I have all along intended sending you at least a few lines by Thomas[1]. You were rather low when I left you — so was I — but we must make the best of things, and I am resolved to shut my eyes on all disagreeables as much as possible. George would tell you it was fair or very nearly so all the way to Halifax. I had no idea of sleeping, and did not pretend to go to bed till eleven thirty. I had a feverish doze or two, and got up at one thirty — the mail was unusually late. I had time to take two cups of coffee, and a glass of cold water, make a very tolerable breakfast; for we were not off till one, that would be a quarter to two by the kitchen. There was only one vacant place inside — three men besides myself — one of them Mr Crossley the carpet-man. It was fair and fine the whole way — a very nice, mild, morning after a rainy boisterous night at Halifax till after twelve. We came in two and a half hours. They were too late to stop and set us down here, and we got out at the Golden Lion and walked. Thomas took one half the luggage while I watched

---

[1] A servant who accompanied Anne to Leeds.

the other, then returned for the rest, and I was comfortably seated here in quarter of an hour. Called up Boots, went with him to three or four doors where he had people to call, knew Marian's voice, and gave her a rousing at a quarter past five — she was already up. I shall go on the box with the Coachman to Selby. It was very hot inside. I was absolutely in a state of humid ardour (?) the whole way — besides the atmosphere was only relieved by a chink of open window first on one side then on the other (seldom both together) and, the atmosphere, before we had done with it, was pretty well *elaborated*.

(Steam packet from Selby, eleven a.m.) I am determined to write a few lines on board to shew you I am not sick, and, besides, to make as much way with my father as I can. I made myself comfortable in a sitting room to myself at Leeds, and, by this means, sat hid from my father and Marian, and had only just time to speak to them as they got into the coach. They walked a mile on the Otley road yesterday evening, and look well and in good spirits this morning. We were off from Leeds precisely at six — I on the box. The fine weather continues — and we had a sufficiently pleasant drive. We are at this moment at Booth ferry, and I must go upon deck to take a peep. I can strap up my desk literally in two minutes.

Twelve thirty pm. We have just passed Saltmarshe, and grounded about ten minutes ago, here, therefore, we are sand-bound for the next two hours to come, and several of the passengers have followed us down into the cabin. Marian is sitting by me mending my glove. Thomas sitting opposite, pressing his finger on the musical box of his neighbour to which about fifteen of us are listening with complacency. I do not look up much, but catch a glance now and then at me and my letter — of wonder, perhaps, at my *comfortability*. The day is delightful, I think you would have enjoyed our voyage. The scenery along the banks is tame, but looks cheerful amid the sunshine, and as pleasant as East Riding can be. Marian is not very loquacious, and her admiration if much excited, not much exprest — but 'tis probably "silence eloquent". Saltmarshe is close upon the water — a three-storied house the four lower windows (eight in front) bayed, and the whole facade covered with ivy, that red-berried creeper (I forget its name) and one thing or other, till not a particle of brick is to be seen. Not so the tiled roof which has a shameless conspicuousness that spoils the whole.

Mr S — was standing by the water's edge superintending some workmen planting. But I must tell you that, leaving Leeds at six, we stopt at the Petre-arms, Selby, at nine, were on board the *Favourite* steam-packet in twenty-five minutes , and weighed in a quarter of an hour. At ten, nine of us (Mr Crossley one) sat down to breakfast — tea, hot muffins, cold ham, and cold bread and butter. All pretty good, but the butter, which was strongish; but we are now, as it were, at sea — at least, the water is salt. We are so completely aground, and our containing element so completely calm, that we are as still as if safely housed in our sitting-room at Shibden. Poor old Shibden! Before, while we were *bona fide* going on *swimmingly*, there was a tremulous sort of motion very strange to me at my writing desk. You perceive I cannot help mentioning my writing desk. Well! Let those laugh who win, and it is a great comfort to me. All the rest are staring at each other, twirling their fingers, &c., &c., for idleness' sake. I am as pleasantly employed as I could possibly be at the London Hotel, Hull. They say it will be six or seven before we get there; and, if the wind be against us we may not reach London till Monday. But it is hoped and expected we shall land on Tower hill about six on Sunday evening. They tell us that the *Yorkshireman* is much more commodious than the *Kingston*, but that the latter is much the better sailer. This is most especially what we want, and 'tis lucky enough as it happens. We shall pass the *Aire and Calder*, Miss Marsh's packet, in the Humber from which we are now some miles distant. There are neither books nor newspapers to be seen here — two or three printed advertisements and a catalogue of books, old and new to be bought at Joseph Noble's, Market Place, Hull, constitute all our stock of literature. By the way, my father called on Mr Widdle in Selby for his road-interest. It was sent to him to Market Weighton only yesterday, and will doubtless be forwarded thence to Shibden. George paid a shilling for me at Miss Kitson's, which, amid the musings of yesterday evening, I quite forgot to repay him. Will you have the goodness to settle this matter for me. Perhaps I am writing you an odd sort of rigmarole; but we shall have little or no time in Hull, and I may as well fill my paper here, and in this manner, as nowhere and not at all. It will shew you how we begin to go on. At this moment I am moved to another table — the other is wanted for dinner. There has been what is called a good smell for some time past, and I am curious to know what sort of dinner it turns out. The k(itchen) is about such another as Madame Joly's. I think we shall all be well enough amused with our journey; yet, notwithstanding, I shall not be sorry when it is over. Some of my neighbours are speculating on the possible chance of our falling in with his Majesty. But there has been a fair wind for him, and they fear he will have got too much start of us. I cannot help wondering what you are all about just now at home — in a bustle, I suppose, and hope; because, possibly, it may rather amuse you than otherwise. I longed to ask you this morning how you slept last night. But I really will leave a little of my paper for a line or two before we go to bed to say how we are likely to find ourselves at the London Hotel, Hull. My father abuses my ink for not drying, and strongly recommends some of Battle's. But somehow or other I cannot, as they say, fancy it. However, I really will wish you goodbye for the present. My father and Marian have been gone on deck this quarter of an hour — I verily believe they are both much pleased.

Hull. Ten p.m. The London Hotel turns out the Shakespeare tavern, Humber Street. It is a very second rate sort of house, but the people are very civil, the beds seem very good, we are near the place of embarkation for London, and, all things considered, perhaps we could not have been better off. We have been on board the *Kingston* to reconnoitre, and taken three sophas by way of beds. I fear the cabin will be very warm, but I trust we shall be at Webb's hotel, Piccadilly, by seven or eight on Sunday. We were aground just three hours and three minutes, just opposite Whitgiff, and landed within a hundred yards of here exactly at seven. We have had a very remarkably fine day. Thomas has really been very attentive and useful, and I have bid him tell you so, and told him how much we are obliged to him. Marian complains of being a little tired. The water was so calm, there was no chance of being sick today; but I am afraid she will be a sufferer tomorrow. We are to be called at five. Thomas will see us off, and I shall then give him this, which I rather fancy you will get on Sunday. So far the account of us all is very good, and I hope to send you one equally so from Calais, or perhaps I shall wait to announce our safe arrival in Paris. I am getting too sleepy to know much about what I am writing, and it will be wise to make all speed to bed. I trust you will go on prosperously. I shall feel much more satisfied after

having had a letter from you. But no more, I can only say goodnight. My father's and Marian's and my own best love, and believe me, my dear aunt, always most affecty yours,
A.L. -

Calais. Saturday evening. 7 September 1822.

You will be a little surprised, my dear aunt, at the date of my letter — Calais instead of Paris — but you shall hear all by and by, and, as I have, of course, a great deal to tell you, suppose we begin and go on regularly. You know all about us up to the morning of this day-week, when Thomas saw us off from Hull in *The Kingston* at six a.m. We had a delightful day, and sailed along very pleasantly till ten or eleven, when Marian became a little sickish, and went to lie down. I was rather unwell for about an hour, but not very bad when I could go on reading the Vicar of Wakefield; and an hour and half's nap in the cabin, set me up for the voyage. My father not sick at all. We had some hope of coming up with his Majesty on his way from Edinburgh,[2] and this kept us all on the lookout. About three thirty in the afternoon we descried two frigates, and we among nineteen of the passengers immediately subscribed 6d. each for porter to enable our four firemen to make a push, and bring us up with the squadron. At five thirty hailed the *Brothers of Sunderland*, and learnt that his Majesty was six miles south of Flambro' Head at six the preceding evening. I staid till ten, and then went below for the night. The cabin was sophaed, or rather benched round, with three tables down the middle, spread over with carpet-covered mattresses and a bolster for each person. We had had the precaution to take one of the side benches as soon as we got to Hull, and were better off than those on the tables. I really slept soundly. It was a curious scene, and laughable enough. On Sunday at four thirty a.m. we all ran on deck to get the first peep at the royal squadron eight or ten miles ahead of us. We had passed the Yarmouth sands from eight to twelve in the evening before, that is fifty miles in four hours. It was a delightful morning, and the sun rose beautifully. The wind was so fair for them, and the *James Watt* steam-packet of Leith had the royal yatch so powerfully in tow, we could gain no ground at sea, but were sure of getting up with them in the river. At nine thirty a.m. we passed the nose (at which the Thames begins) and at ten thirty came alongside and gave the King three-times-three as hearty cheers as John Bull ever gave in his life. The salutes from the shipping — the thunder of artillery from Tilbury-fort, Woolwich, &c. the shouts of the people — the fine day — the King's band and the Lord Mayor's — the altogether — formed a scene impressively grand, and with which, as you may imagine, we were all most delighted. We were close alongside the royal yatch when she cast anchor opposite to Greenwich hospital, and had an excellent view of his Majesty. He smiled most graciously, bowed most elegantly, looked in good spirits, well, and handsome. Had we not loitered in the train of royalty, we could have got to London by one or two; but, as it was, we made the best of our way from Greenwich thro' the crowds of boats (wonderful no accident happened) and landed at tower stairs at six. The sail up the Thames is beautiful, and well worth two or three hours' sickness. Surely, the hotel des Invalides at Paris will not bear comparison with Greenwich hospital. However, one thing or other took up time, and it was seven before we were safely landed in Piccadilly. Mrs Webbe had all ready, and we felt quite at home immediately — we had a sitting-room and three lodging rooms (one of them the one you had) all close together. There were two packets to sail for Calais; the *Talbot* on Tuesday, the *Lord Neville*, much the finer and better of the two, on Wednesday, and this, in the first instance, made us determine not to go till the latter day. On Monday we went to Hammersley's, ordered about one passport, and walked along the Bird-cage walk, past where Sir William Fawcett[3] used first to live, &c., &c. On Tuesday we set out about half past ten, and walked *really* thirteen or fourteen miles before dinner at five thirty. We were almost all over the city, St Martin's le grand, &c., &c. My uncle would not know again the place where Mr Whiteley used to live. Saw St Paul's, the court of the British Museum (the museum itself shut now), the Squares, bridges, St Martin's Church, Exeter 'change, Westminster Abbey, Burlington Arcade, Western Exchange Bazar, &c., &c. By the way I bought you a very pretty little, tasty, basket containing a hundred gold-eyed needles (of different sizes) as a present for Madame Joly — price 2s. so that you will see your thimble again at no great expense. Tho' it is only three years since your being in town, you would scarce know again the region about Carlton Palace, and from Piccadilly to

Portland Place now terminated by Park-crescent. I exprest more astonishment at all these wonderful improvements than Marian has ever done ever since our leaving home. She sees everything, as you thought she would, very quietly; and no multiplicity of remark betrays her want of experience. London would now be nearly as new to my uncle, as if he had never been there. All was changed to my father — the Bird-cage walk, everything with a new face on. From Regent's Crescent (close to Webb's Hotel, opening into Regent's Street, and on to Carlton Palace) to Portland Place, terminated by Park-crescent, looking on Regent's Park, is now, surely, the finest street in Europe. I walked, and as I walked, gazed in amazement. They are beginning to attend to ornament as well as comfort in building. They are making London what it ought to be, and piazzas, colonnades, and all the beautiful &c. of finished architecture are starting up in Roman cement. You would not know the Haymarket again. But no more — I must hasten to other things. Till Tuesday afternoon we knew not but of going in the *Lord Melville*; but the conductor of the French diligence-concern happening to come to us about the passport, persuaded my father to book himself for Paris in *L'hirondelle*, and we drove off for Dover ten minutes before eight on Wednesday morning. A delightful day smiled upon us, and we were set down at the London hotel, close to the quay and custom-house at Dover, at six thirty in the evening. What tricks time plays! All is changed within these three years about the swallow — a new line of Inn — a new description of carriage, four wheels instead of two — but hung low, and still boasting of its superior safety. Marian confessed herself struck with the prospect from Boughton-hill — the hop-grounds looked beautiful — women were gathering the flowers — the martins had deserted the sand-hill just out of Gravesend. The Gothic cottage I admired so much at Sittingbourne is now intruded on by other Gothic cottages, and looks not half as retired as it did. I got Miss Vallance's letter which I am much obliged to you for forwarding. She fancied we should pass thro' Sittingbourne as yesterday, would take care to be at home, and begged very kindly and attentively to see us. I must write to her as soon as we are settled in Paris. To return, however, to our travels, we embarked on board the *Dasher* Steam-packet at Dover at eleven fifteen on Thursday. All changed again — nothing but steam-packets now — scarce once

61

in six or twelve months a common vessel comes over — the mail, and travellers, all brought by steam. We were just two hours and fifty-five minutes from embarking at Dover to landing on the pier here. The wind was high, the sea rough, and the spray like a shower of rain the whole way. Marian did not know it was not 'thick, misty rain' till I told her this morning. It spoilt my hat completely; for I did not like to stay below — such a sick scene as the cabin I never beheld. Not a single passenger escaped sickness but my father, who has been obliged the pay the penalty on land. We should have gone forwards at eight yesterday morning; but he was too bilious to bear moving — what I should call a regular sick headache — he is coming about again, and we hope to be off on Monday. I was surprised to find him so much better sailor than the rest, and feared from the first, he must make up for it afterwards. In crossing we shipt a sea repeatedly, and the vessel laboured so, we could none of us stand. The pitching — going up, and then sinking down, gave me exactly the feeling of descending from the height in a swing. The coach concern being so altered, we should have gone not to Meurices, but to the London hotel. I was for trying Oakeshott's, and most fortunately; for it is an excellent house, where we have too many English comforts to make us feel that we are in France. I have never yet been able to fancy us really at Calais. We have a most comfortable sitting-room, and three equally comfortable lodging-rooms close adjoining — capital cooking superintended by an English housekeeper — cold roast beef, veal &c. as in England. Soups, not like dish-washings, but real essences of meat — salmon from London — beef from Flanders, merino mutton, small and excellent. Oakeshott prides himself on his wines — and the *vin du pays* is certainly very far superior to any I ever tasted before. He is much employed by gentlemen to send them wine to England, he answers for safe arriving in London. But the prices keep pace with the quality, of course, and the very best Burgundy, he says, will cost about thirteen shillings a bottle before it is safe in London — very best Champagne 10/6 — Chablis, Sauterne, vin de Grave, seven or eight shillings or not quite so much. My father has been obliged to live on tea and soup, but Marian and I have dined at the table d'hote at four or half-past — Fish and soup, and then two complete courses of really good things, and then dessert. For instance, within sight of Marian and me today, after gravy soup, salmon, and stewed eels, was a fine piece of roast beef, stewed pigeons, fricasséed cauliflower, most excellent sweetbread pâté, *something* larded, boiled potatos, fricasséed chicken, boiled tongue. 2d. course partridges, capital sweet omelet, plum tart, &c. Now, positively for all this we are charged a franc less than they charged us at Boulogne for the b.g. concern — ie. we only pay three francs. I would far rather be here than at Dessin's — Quillac has made money enough, and given up the hotel to Dessin, grandson, I believe to the Dessin that kept this house, the Silver Lion, when Sterne was here some sixty years ago. The butcher's shop part of our hotel was standing in Sterne's time, the rest has been rebuilt only about thirty years ago, and is now the most convenient, and, I think, altogether the prettiest hotel in Calais; and I went out this morning, and took great pains to see all the best of them. Marian staid with my father while I reconnoitred the town for two and a half hours. I then returned for her, and we watched the turn-out of the Mailpacket (the *Dasher* that we came in on Thursday), for a sight of the Duke of Wellington and Lord Clanwilliam, expected to pass thro' on their way to the Congress.[4] However, they are not arrived. She seems most amused with some women crying pears. She thinks the women's caps 'frightful', and the potatos too long and sweet, and bespeaking that the people do not know how to cultivate them. These, I believe, are all the observations I have heard her make. But I shall not write more tonight because I wish to leave a little of my paper for tomorrow. By the way George paid Miss Kitson a shilling for me the night I came away, which I forgot to repay him — I think I mentioned it in my last:- but my father gave him a shilling to pay the postage of the 2d. letter to Mr Webb, which he (George) must have forgotten to do; as the postage of this letter was charged in our bill. Now this shilling will go to pay for Miss Kitson.

---

[2] George IV's good reception in Dublin, in 1821, encouraged him to visit Edinburgh in August 1822. This was the first royal visit since 1650.

[3] General Sir William Fawcett, son of Martha Fawcett (née Lister) was born at Shibden Hall in 1727. He had a distinguished military career, fighting in the 1745 Rebellion, in the campaign in Flanders in 1746 and 1748, and in the Seven Years' War, 1756-63. Before his death (in 1804) he became virtual Commander of the British army. His letters are in the Shibden Hall collection.

[4] Congress of Vienna, 20 October 1822.

Monday morning. 9 September 1822. We are not off yet, my dear aunt, nor do I exactly know when we shall be. Not having gone forwards immediately, we are obliged to wait for places, and may not have them till Wednesday or Thursday, there is so much travelling, and so very many people afloat. Two or three packets full seem to come in daily. My father is going on as well as can be, and seems fully sensible of all the comforts we have here. You can judge from experience how a bowel-complaint weakens one. I took a couple of pills as soon as we got to London, and Marian took magnesia, and we have both been quite well. But you know my father, and can easily imagine that to the teaspoonful of magnesia (not half enough) he was persuaded to take a few hours after landing here, he attributes all his pain and sickness. However, it is over now — be it as it may, I shall never perhaps venture to recommend medicine to him in future, and can only hope that his plan of leaving nature entirely to herself, will always answer as well as the strength of his constitution has made it do now. He desires me to say, our sitting-room is covered with a handsome Brussels carpet — it is about six yards by six-and-a-half, and very comfortably furnished in the English-French style. The sopha has been a great comfort to my father, but he has given up wanting it now. By the way, we had a bottle of Chambertin Burgundy yesterday which might be delivered in London at ten shils a bottle, very good indeed. We have had excellent Sauterne, too. But neither my father nor Marian seem to care much about these, or the *vin du pays*, the only three wines we have called for as yet. It was Sauterne that you and I took with us from Paris to Rouen, and that we both liked so much, the next best to Hermitage. We breakfast at ten, and Marian has always been ready. I was out early this morning — passed the four draw-bridges to Low Calais about a mile off, and, after reading the inscriptions on the tombstones and black-painted crosses in the church-yard, went in to matins. Only two women, a young man, and a child there, besides myself. I enjoyed my walk very much — the people are all afloat at five or six o'clock. By and by, when I have put this into the post-office, I am going to take Marian onto the pier and then onto the sands which seem extensive and good. The pier must (from my walking) be five or six hundred yards long. It was so windy yesterday, I thought I should have been blown off, and was obliged to return before

I had got to the end, whence the Dover coast and castle are very distinctly seen. The Duke of Wellington is expected today. I frequently walk out by myself; for Marian's heel is not *quite* well, and it would be foolish not to take care of it for Paris. I have now reconnoitred the town here thoroughly, and think it a very nice place — plenty of bustle on the quays when the packets come in — several English families living here, but none of them cut much figure at church yesterday. Service began at half-past eleven in a room fitted up for the purpose in the street (Rue Neuve) — there was no attempt made at singing, but the clergyman, an elderly man, did the duty very well. A family of eleven is just gone — and as soon as another packet arrives the rooms will be full again. I will write as soon as we are a little settled in Paris. In the mean time, if you have anything particular to say, direct Poste Restante à Paris. My father and Marian join me in best love to yourself and my uncle. Marian declares she has nothing to say, but will write to you when we have been a little while in Paris. Marian all out about the potatos — they set them here with manure as they do in England; but Marian is not yet convinced they understand how to grow them. Not a pudding since we came. Marian says my letter is as long as a sermon. Tell me if (you) can read it — my father and Marian both say you cannot — mention what day you receive it. Marian ate her last bun here on Thursday night. She turns up her nose at all the French carriages, and my father laughs. I have only room to add I am always, my dear aunt, very affecty yours, A.L. -

The Listers cut short their visit to Paris on account of Captain Lister's illness. He wished to return home, being quite disenchanted with France, and with the idea that he and Marian might take up residence there, after the sale of their estate at Market Weighton.

6

SOCIAL LIFE IN PARIS

1824

On 24 August 1824 Miss Lister travelled by coach to London, the first stage of her journey to Paris. There she intended to spend a few months, for the sake of her health and to improve her knowledge of the French language. Her letters to her aunt, in their detailed descriptions, perfectly re-create the life of the times. Many of the things on which she comments have been taken for granted by other travellers of the period, and consequently have been left unrecorded.

220 Piccadilly. Friday morning 27 August 1824.

Never, my dear aunt, was anyone more favoured with weather. Up to this time, (eight thirty a.m.), we have not had one cloudy half hour. We got to Leeds at half past nine — had a 2d. breakfast, and were off for London exactly at twelve. The country looks beautiful, and I enjoyed my place on the box with the coachman, exceedingly. Among our numerous party, were four pointer-dogs which travelled in the boot, without exciting further observation than that they were quarreling, and making a great noise. Poor animals! it was their last effort to escape suffocation; and, on looking at them half way between Pontefract and Doncaster, three were taken out quite dead, the fourth not likely to recover. Got to Doncaster at four. The bridge-house was Graham's academy, the carpet manufactory being in the adjoining buildings. The church-steeple struck me as very handsome. On stopping at the Old Angel, whom should I meet on the stairs, but Mrs Wilcock, and her daughters. She knew me better (than) I knew her. She had brought her oldest daughter to school, and was on the point of setting off home. Miss Pickford quite well — at Oxford. Got to Newark at half past eight, Stamford at two on Wednesday morning, breakfasted at Eaton Socon (the Inn a very pretty one) at half past six, took a hackney coach from Islington, and arrived here at three. Mr Webb and his servants all in deep mourning for Mrs Webb who died two months ago — after suffering a very great deal from a cancer in the womb — the house exceedingly altered, and improved. I have a very nice sitting-room and bedroom, and a room for Cordingley close to mine. Poor Cordingley! She was quite well as far as Stamford (it was a beautiful night), but soon afterwards (I am persuaded it was owing to her tasting the guard's brandy and water at Stamford!) began to be very bilious, and sick, and fit for nothing but bed. However, she was so much better yesterday morning, as to be glad to get out with me, and walk ten or twelve miles — was a little tired, but seems not a jot the worse for it this morning. Yet her being so sick, gave me rather a fright of trying her strength in the *Lord Melville*; and I at once determined to have places from here, via Dover, to Paris. We shall be off on Sunday morning at seven, sleep at Dover, cross the next day, and sleep at Quillac's (the Silver Lion, Lion d'Argent), and get to Paris about eight on Wednesday evening. I did a great deal yesterday — ordered and paid for your tea and my father's; and they promised that both should be sent off today, with the receipts enclosed. When in Monument-yard thought it a pity not to let Cordingley see at least the outside of the tower, and therefore walked round it. Went to the Guildhall, to St Paul's during service, to some Squares, and to the bazar, &c. Asked Cordingley how she liked London — she thinks it a very grand place, but should be tired of it in a month. It is indeed a magnificent city, fit for the metropolis of the world. Like Tyre of old, her merchants are princes. What an immense population! About 4,000 refugees, chiefly Spanish, settled in the neighbourhood of Soho Square about a year ago.[1] What buildings! What shops! You must come again, by and by, to see the improvements. I am as busy as a bee — not ever

---

[1] After the restoration of Ferdinand of Spain, November 1823.

on the wing, but ever on the foot. I am going again today, to try if I cannot get to see the tread-mill (Clerkenwell — I must have permission from the sitting magistrate in Hatton Garden, and was too late (after three) yesterday). The worst of it is the heat of the weather; but I can bear it as well as most people.

Friday evening. I had a long walk, my dear aunt, this morning, and am too tired to write much tonight. Went all along Holborn, and Cheapside, which seems to be literally, from the prices marked in the windows, the best place for cheap bargains. Strolled along Gray's Inn — musing as I passed the chambers of Messrs. Brougham, Denman, &c., &c. Made a point of walking along St Martins le Grand. One side, at *this end near Newgate St, will be grand*, when the new post-office is finished. The walls of the underground story are just raised even with the ground, forming an odd-looking collection of variously formed and variously sized compartments. From here went along Cheapside, down Queen Street to the new iron bridge (the Southwark bridge) a very handsome one — finished soon after you and I were here. Foot passengers pay a penny-toll. The new London bridge is to be a little above (a little to the west of) the old one. Sauntered leisurely home — then examined some of the buildings in this quarter. Strolled along the Burlington Arcade, and had my hair cut by the said-to-be best in London, Truefitt, New Bond St. I think Parsons of York does it quite as well. No more ringlets, and cork-screw curls — large curls, not too low on the face. Long waists certainly. The walking-about people wear from few to many flounces. I have not seen one cap that struck me as particularly suitable to you, tho' I have stared at all in my way. I never saw a place so improved; and, literally, I am quite at home here — so amused, I have had no time to find out professor Coleman. You know, I did not exactly like the letter; but it shall lie by me, to be used, or nor, as may seem good and convenient on my return. If you see Mr S -, merely say, I was much obliged to him, but had written you word, I was too much engaged to have even one spare hour. Wright, the wine-merchant, is all a puff — pays nine-hundred a year for advertisements, and makes it answer, tho' never gets the same customer a second time. 'You cannot have good wine', says Mr Webbe, 'without employing a thoroughly respectable merchant, and paying a good price, for instance, £3 a dozen — Griffiths is the man.' But I am now drinking very good old port of which Mr Webbe himself would let my uncle have any quantity at £3 a dozen. Now this I know to be worth the money — better than that we had at Penrith — one would not be ashamed to give it to anyone. Tell Marian, with my love, I went this morning to the shop where Mr W — bought her pencil, and find it cost 10/- exclusive of 3/- for the case of black lead to replenish with. I could not help smiling at the thought of Mr W's saying he had not money enough to see all the exhibitions. I have adopted his plan, and for his own reason, or one might be tempted to death. I went into Fleet-market this morning, and looked up at the Prison. Only one grate by which the debtors can look out towards the street (the market), and ask charity for the poor debtors who have no allowance. Thought I to myself, merry as Mr Mitchell used to say they were, thank Heaven, I am not there.

Quillac's Hotel, Calais. Monday evening. 30 August. Saturday night and last night I really was so tired and sleepy, I could not write to you, my dear aunt, even one line. Walking about all day on Saturday — travelling from London to Dover yesterday — the Jews' synagogue in Denmark-court is a poor dirty shabby place, far below the synagogue you and I were at in Paris. The tread-mill very much worth seeing. I got upon it for two or three minutes, and have nothing to say against it — cannot imagine how it can do any harm.

Miss Lister's visit to the tread-mill was reported in *The Times* of 28 August, 1824:

Police.

Hatton-Garden. A lady, whose address and habiliments bespoke her of foreign extraction, appeared before the Magistrates to prefer a request for an order to view the tread-mill at Cold Bathfields prison. The singularity of the application, and the no less unique manner of the applicant, made Mr Rogers pause before he replied. The lady again repeated her request.
Magistrate — Is it any of the confined you wish to see, Madam?
Applicant — No, Sir.
Magistrate — Is yours, then, merely a visit of

inspection?

Applicant — Yes, Sir; just so.

Magistrate — The proper person to obtain orders from are the visiting Magistrates; and neither I, nor my brother Justice on the bench, are visiting Magistrates.

Applicant — I made application at the prison, and was referred to the Magistrates of this office.

Magistrate — We may, certainly, grant you an order; but do you go alone?

Applicant — Yes; surely in a metropolitan prison there is nothing indelicate or offensive — nothing, I presume, which a female might not, with the strictest regard to propriety or decorum, inspect.

Magistrate — Certainly nothing indelicate is permitted; but your request is rather singular. May I take the liberty of asking, do you come from the country?

Applicant — Yes, Sir; and as I stay not very long, I am anxious to see everything worth seeing. Indeed, I was particularly desirous to see this tread-mill.

Magistrate — What name shall we grant an order for?

Applicant — Miss Lyster, if you please, Sir.

The fair applicant was just then proceeding to state something of a more particular nature, with respect to the motive that led her to examine this machine, when Mr Laing ordered the office to be cleared. It turned out, that Miss Lyster was actuated by a worthier motive than mere curiosity in making the request, which was ultimately granted by Mr Rogers.

Miss Lister's letter continued: The country of Dover looked beautiful — the hops promising an abundant crop. I took Cordingley with me this morning to the castle at Dover. It was a very broiling walk, but repaid one's trouble. A ducking in a horse-pond could not have moistened one much more. Embarked on board the *Britannia* steam packet at twelve — an hour before we got out of the harbour. Landed on the quay here at four. A beautiful day — fine cool breezes in our favour, and the sea as smooth as glass, nobody sick, not even Cordingley. Masters and mistresses are excused the searching, but servants must undergo it, and poor Cordingley went with two or three more. However, they did not detain her long. I have observed no sign of wishing herself back again, as yet. Calais is exceedingly improved within these two years, and Quillac has made the Hotel look better than it did in Oakeshott's time. The contrast between our side of the water and this, is by no means so striking now, as it was when my father and Marian were here, much less when you were here five years ago. They are laying causeways in the streets. We have had beautiful weather ever since leaving you — a drop or two of rain just before we landed, but no more till just now, when it is raining heavily, thundering loudly and lightning so vividly and perpetually, Cordingley has just come down to me to say, she dares not sit by herself, 'it lightens so hard, and the candle seems to catch it'. Do tell Marian they have been crying pears to her heart's content. I thought of her the instant I heard the well-known cry. They have sent the trunks from the custom-house, so completely turned inside out, they will have to be entirely repacked; and I begin to feel sleepy. There will be no post from here tomorrow but the Captn of our packet has promised to call for my letters, and put them in at Dover in time for tomorrow night's Dover post, that I hope you will get this on Saturday. Cordingley makes no complaints, and seems quite well. I have already begun to eat fruit, tho' not grapes. Have had soup à la Julienne, fricassée de poulet, kidney beans and, do tell Marian, potatos she could not know from English, and excellent bread and butter, and red hermitage, and pears and apricots. The pier is greatly enlarged. I am writing in a hurry, wanting to pack and go to bed — am sitting in and have dined in my bedroom (in the French fashion), a very neat and pretty room on the opposite side of the house to where my father and Marian were. I think of you all much oftener than you fancy, and shall think of you on Wednesday. Shall leave here between nine and ten tomorrow get into Paris about eight and perhaps to Monsr de B(oyve)'s by nine. I feel better than I expected, and shall feel quite satisfied when I have had one letter from you of good tidings. My best love to you all, my dear aunt, very affecty yours

A.L. -

Cordingley sends her duty. Tuesday morning 31 August. Not bit once in London — my eyes blocked up this morning tho' my room remarkably neat, and pretty, and comfortable and the first floor from the ground. In a hurry — ever my dear aunt affecty yours. If the Captn on the *Britannia* does not call in time, I shall put my letter into the post-office, and you will be a day longer in getting it.

Paris. Place Vendôme 24. Wednesday 8 September 1824.

My last letter, my dear aunt, which I hope you would receive about last Sunday, would tell you all my proceedings up to the time of my leaving Calais, yesterday-week. We had a very prosperous, but exceedingly hot, and latterly rather dusty journey, tho', fortunately, the heavy rain at Calais had so laid the dust for the first half the way, that, considering the time of year, we shd make no complaint on this score. Yet the heat surpassed anything I ever felt. Tho' only three of us in the cabriolet, and all the windows down, the sun's rays, darting full upon us, were more broiling than you can imagine. In, and on the coach, there were twenty people and, surely, it would not have been possible to muster half as many dry threads of linen. Yet everybody bore the journey apparently well — Cordingley not at all sick. It was past ten before we got off from Calais, and more than half past eleven when we got here. (Friday morning 10 September 1824.) A visit from Madame de B(oyve) interrupted me on Wednesday, and yesterday, my dear aunt, I was out all the day — today is the ninth since our arrival; and, with one thing or other, I have only just had time to keep my accounts and journal. We breakfast at any hour we choose in our rooms, there is luncheon at one, and we dine about six, tho' the hour is called half past five. There is no doing anything after dinner. We have had company every evening, more or less. But this is the very thing for me: it shews one French manners, and style of conversation, of which, I find, all is impossible to learn by living at an hotel as you and I did, is a mere nothing. I have already given up the idea of attempting to improve myself in anything but French, and, *perhaps*, Italian; because the person of whom I mean to have lessons in the former, will, if I am a favourite, give me valuable instructions in the latter, gratis. She is an Italian Countess whose estates were confiscated by Napoleon, in part of payment of the immense defalcation of public money occasioned by her run-away husband, the Count de Galvani[2] — is recommended by

Lady Dacre who has so beautifully translated several of Petrarch's sonnets, speaks French like a scholar, and a woman of fashion, and will, I trust, do me a great deal of good. The society we see here is very good. By and by we shall begin to have parties of fifty or sixty, to go more to the theatres, &c., &c., and I really must muster French enough to carry me well thro' general conversation. Luckily for me, Madame de B(oyve) seems to have taken a fancy to me; and I like to be as much with her as I can: as all our present party in the house are English, and seldom speak French except to Madame. On my arrival, I found here Mr and Mrs Brande, from a very handsome house in Arlington Street, London. He is apothecary to the King and royal family and brother to Professor Brande of the Royal Institution. They left us on Tuesday morning on their tour to Germany. A Mr (John Baring) Short, a naval offcer, as I suppose, and from Exeter, left us on Wednesday for Brussels. He is 2d. cousin to the Shorts of George Street Westminster, whom you have heard Isabella mention, and 1st cousin to the Barings. We have still left a Mrs Mackenzie, a widow (and her daughter *aetatis* sixteen) whose husband (Mr Mackenzie) was paymaster general at Calcutta; and a Mrs Barlow, and her daughter *aetatis* thirteen. Mrs B. — also a widow. Her husband commanded the 61st regt at the battle of Salamanca, and was killed there. Mrs B. — is ladylike; and her connections seem very good.

Letter from Anne Lister, in Paris, to her aunt at Shibden Hall, 29 October 1824.

. . . Accident yesterday made my friend Mrs Barlow acquainted with the real cause of my being here.[3] Her kindness and advice have made an impression on me, which, I trust, it is impossible that I should ever be so ungrateful as to forget. She begged me to consult — I have taken the earliest opportunity of doing so, and am only this moment returned. He says much that is

---

[2] Luigi de Galvani (1737-1798), Italian physiologist after whom galvanism received its name.

[3] On account of her health; she was secretly having treatment for a virus infection.

satisfactory, but wishes to see me again in seven or eight days, before he can give his opinion decidedly. I have weighed the circumstances very carefully; for I know that the probable delay of two or three weeks in my return, will be a disappointment to you, if it be not amply recompensed by the good to be attained by it — but should my hopes be realized, I am quite sure you will think I have determined well. The purpose of my journey will then be answered; and I shall then endeavour to forget, as soon as I can, all the discomforts I have endured. You shall hear from me again immediately after my next seeing -, when I shall be able to tell you something more certain. I am writing in a great hurry with a thousand fears of being still too late for today's post — if so, my letter cannot go till Wednesday. My best love to yourself, and my uncle, and my father and Marian. It makes me quite comfortable and satisfied to hear such good accounts. Ever, my dear aunt, most affecty yours,
A.L. -
Paris, Place Vendôme 24. Tuesday night 7 December 1824.

I really could not write, my dear aunt, by yesterday's post. I was detained so long, I could not get back in time to write even half a dozen lines. You will of course be anxious to hear the result — the advice is very different from that I have had given before, and, at least sounds better. I am to leave off what I have hitherto tried, and adopt a new system — the whys and wherefores I shall not think of attempting to explain till my return home — the plan will give me a great deal of trouble. I am to take a warm bath for an hour every other day, &c., &c., &c., but I find it is time to do something decided; and I only hope you and my uncle will be satisfied that I am judging wisely. Say the best you can to my father and Marian — tell them my anxiety to improve myself in French. And do not, my dear aunt, even fidget yourself for one moment. I do assure you, I have not been in such good spirits these three years, and have nothing to say that is not satisfactory. I am told to take a month. All things considered, this seems hardly enough; but it is impossible to say as yet. My only anxiety is about Cordingley. Perhaps I may send her back; for I can do quite well without her. But I shall do nothing till I hear from you again. Mrs Barlow will allow her servant to do all for me I want. I cannot say much now; but believe me (and I would really tell you truly, were it otherwise) you have not the smallest reason for the smallest disquietude about me, in any way. Could you know half the kindness and attention of my friend Mrs B. -, you would be quite satisfied. I do not want a nurse. All the party think me looking much the better for my stay here — but if I did, I know not a better. My only astonishment is at her liking me well enough to take so much interest and trouble for a person with whom her acquaintance has been so short. But my good fortune always finds me good friends; and I only hope I shall always know how to value and deserve them .... . Now that I cannot go out quite so much as usual, I feel a little more idle; and have, besides, little to say for myself. I see from Galignani's paper[4], that York minster has been lighted with gas, and that Lord Middleton has built a handsome Gothic church at Birdsall. I have read, too, the whole account of Mr Fauntleroy &c., &c., but, as to what occurs here, one knows as little as if one lived at Johnny Groat's house, unless one goes out, and reads the journals.

---

[4] *Galignani's Messenger*, an English daily newspaper, published in Paris from 1814-1904, by Giovanni Galignani, who also founded an English library there in 1800.

Shibden Hall house-body showing fifteenth and
sixteenth century windows

('House-body' meaning 'hall' or 'living-room' is still used
in parts of the West Riding.)

By courtesy of the Metropolitan Borough of Calderdale, Libraries
Department, Northgate, Halifaxe.

7

THE RETURN TO SHIBDEN
— HALIFAX AFFAIRS

Views on Education; The Ladies of Llangollen.

Letter from Anne Lister at Shibden Hall to Sibbella Maclean at Edinburgh. 1 May 1825.

. . . Now that you understand me better, do you not agree, few characters are more mistaken than my own, even by those who seem on terms of intimacy with me. How happens this? I rarely meet with those who *interest* me, who have the charm that brings me back to that disguised, and hidden nature, that suits not with the world. 'I could be much that I have not been',[1] Had it been my fate to meet in early life, with one whose disposition exactly corresponded with my own, whose heart could beat with a regard as warm, as constant, as devoted, I should have been much better, and much happier. But 'the heart knoweth its own bitterness'; and bitter indeed are the first moments of that conviction which tells us, we have missed the good we sought, and must be hopeless to find it ever. All afterwards is turned to doubt. Confidence is gone. We mistrust even ourselves, and fear to judge a second time. Will you read this with surprise; or is it your own opinion with which time has made you so familiar, that it seems not strange from anyone? We will talk of all this when we meet . . . .

---

[1] Sentences in single quotes are quotations from Anne's letter to Sibbella Maclean.

Wednesday afternoon 4 May. I steal an hour for you, while the workmen are at dinner. I have really been very well since my return home; and *rest* is not required, save for the opportunity of once more spending my time as I like. I have not a moment to spare for reading, scarcely one for writing. Yet still, I shall not be 'delighted to find my paper filled — glad of an excuse not to cross'; for the thus having a letter to you in progress, is a relief to the occupations imposed by duty rather than by inclination. We tried, last year, to divert a footpath that is a great nuisance to us. An ill-natured opposition obliged us to give it up at that time; but we shall bring it on next July, and, after having spared nothing that money can do, hope to succeed by dint of proving that the new path is better than the old one. We are, therefore, cutting down hills, and making a raised way across a valley. As my uncle is not able to stir out beyond the garden, and unwilling to have anything done without me (in fact, I am plotter, and planner, and superintendant; and the whole thing is solely to please me), you can imagine my wish not to throw away my uncle's money for nothing, and that my time is completely given up to workmen. I am generally out soon after six in the morning, and, except for an hour at breakfast, only come in in time to dress for dinner at six thirty. I then endeavour to amuse my uncle, and aunt, and go to bed (go to my room) sufficiently tired at ten. Now marvel, Sibbella, as I do myself, that I am thus soon again writing you such a letter as this. After all, I write in more comfort than I did in Paris — that very thin paper, and the perpetual thought that the people at the post-office had a right to read, and might read my letters whenever they chose, were a sort of tiresome restraint, more tiresome than one easily imagines, without experience. Add to these the very weak state I was in at one time, and you will not wonder at my writing in less comfort then, than now. 'What good reason can you give me for not acknowledging your illness to your friends now?' My uncle and aunt know of it; and is not this enough? Mrs Lawton, too, knows of it; for she entered into the suspicion of *undue fascination*. Why tell others? I seldom mention illness, when I can avoid it. I like not to be pitied, or inquired after, except by those very chosen few, among whom I shall always place yourself . . . I went with some friends to see fashions just arrived from Paris &c., &c., and I have seen people wear them. I used to battle it with Miss Norcliffe, that the English ladies understood dress as well as the French — 'tis probable I shall never think so again. Your cousin is naturally stylish and elegant; but the more we see of the world, the more we see of the mere surface of different countries, the more our minds are enlarged, and the more our natural advantages are developed. *Raideur* strikes me as a word of rather difficult explanation: it is not exactly stiffness, not exactly primness, not exactly shyness, but an indescribable compound of all three; it is certainly not 'some sort of gaucherie', not near so bad as the very mildest species of it. In fact, if I could have translated the word into any corresponding term in English, I should have done so, holding in abomination the too common practice of torturing our own fine language with alien words not half so good as ours. A regular quotation now and then, very occasionally, is a different thing, and may be excused; but the jargon of English and French so commonly written, and spoken nowadays, makes me sigh even for the *culpes* and Latinisms of the days of Queen Elizabeth. (*Culpe* from the word *Culpa*, a fault, an odd-sounding but favourite Latinism of Queen Elizabeth, who begged that her people would not impute to her the *culpes* of her parliament vid. Lord Somer's tracts.) Well! but I do not find the word *raideur* in my old French dictionary; and my new one is not yet arrived. How can the English have a word to express that of which they are not conscious, any more than the French to express that *comfort* of which they knew nothing till they borrowed the word, and, with it, some faint idea of its meaning, from us? Sibbella, it would least of all become me to be 'very saucy to my *untravelled* countrywomen'. I, who have scarcely left the threshold of my own sequestered home, should write more modestly. Perhaps, when I have travelled more, I shall do so, like all who have observed, and learnt more solidly. Do not, however, fancy me hardy enough to begin any experiments upon you; tho' it might, nevertheless, be an excellent 'tack' for me, who might be the teacher taught, and, in the idle search for your *raideur*, might lose some little of my own. But I do know you 'like occasionally to teaze' me; and, as none can do it so agreeably, you shall have full licence.

Sunday morning. 8 May. I have kept my letter all this while, Sibbella merely to fill the paper; and, literally, I have not been able to do this, since Wednesday. After talking a little to my uncle and aunt, I am so tired and sleepy in an evening, writing is out of the question. But, surely, this tyranny will pass by about the middle of July, and then I hope to be at liberty. I shall, always, however, be more or less busy at home; for everything falls upon me; and being obliged to go as nearly as possible in the old routine, puts it out of my power to manage things as expeditiously as I wish. My aunt is far from well — gouty and rheumatic and in a state of much debility. I anxiously look forward to her being better when the fine, summer weather comes. My uncle is pretty well when he sits quietly at home, but cannot bear the least exertion. I really begin to feel more and more the cares of the world, and to long for some person always at my elbow, as my Fancy could describe. I am not much calculated to live alone, nor even in society without some tie whose nearness is near as heart and interest can make it. Mrs B(arlow) nursed me so attentively, and so kindly, and even habit had made her so necessary to me, I left her with all the regret you can imagine. But the climate, too, had really some portion of my lament; it certainly suits me rather better than this. But what matters it? I am well — 'home is home', and I am happy. By the way, do you know any picture-fanciers? I can tell you of a holy family, by Titian, a country-party scene by Giorgioni, and an adoration of the magi by Lucas of Holland, all three to be bought cheap, for the twelve hundred francs. The duties of the day interfere with letter-writing, and I have but a moment or two left . . . .

Shibden. Monday afternoon. 23 May 1825.

On coming into breakfast this morning, I found your letter, Sibbella, on my writing-desk. I am now come in for an hour while the people dine, and am determined to enjoy this time in scribbling to you. A half-finished letter to my friend Mademoiselle de Sans is thrown aside; and two epistles, crying out most loudly to be answered, must wait till I have thanked you for yours. There is more partiality than justice in this, but I shall make you judge and jury in the business, and submit to the verdict of no other court. How we may meet, I know not; for my fort is not in meetings, but that 'when next we part, it may be with indifference', I confidently believe will not be the case — to me it seems to be, and, probably, it is impossible. Even should our fancies have wrought but foolishness in thus

linking us together by the charities of epistolary intercourse, the disappointment, on my part at least, would be too signal to be compatible with indifference . . . Oh! that I could make you like myself, dream not at all, or only that which gives pleasure. Do not mistake me. I merely mean by this, that, when I do dream, when I do live at all out of the sphere of reality I take care to do it agreeably, agreeing always with St Matthew, that 'Sufficient till the day, is the evil thereof'. In fact, Sibbella, the study of my latter days had been the attainment of that mindly prudence, which never disquieteth itself in vain . . . I laughed aloud on reading your sentence of excommunication against the foot-path — 'directing — finding fault — a manner is so imperceptibly acquired'. Your expectations of seeing 'a Yorkshire road-maker in the shape of your friend' amuses me exceedingly — this sentence is invaluable. I shall copy it into a conspicuous part of my journal, and read it every day by way of antidote. Why do you call it 'terribly impudent'? It is terribly just; but, luckily for me, I have sense enough to know it. In good truth, and soberness, I thank you for the sentence with all my heart — you never wrote a better, or a kinder . . . I am tanned as brown, as if I had been dyed with walnut-juice . . . Your letters are really a great pleasure to me; and I have great pleasure in answering them. Whether they are what you call 'plain *matter of fact*' or not, they always please me, and their interest, so far from decreasing, improves progressively from page to page. 'Who do you suppose could sit at your elbow from six in the morning to six at night?' None. But less than this, Sibbella, would satisfy the heart of your affectionately attached,
A.L. -

Draft of a letter to Mrs Maria Barlow, in Paris.

Shibden. Thursday afternoon. 26 May 1825.

Your letter, Maria, is lying open before me (it arrived this morning); and I am musing how to methodize my thoughts, and give them written shape. I am delighted your aunt and cousins are arrived; and my heart aches to find your health so delicate, your mind so troubled with anxieties. If it be possible to alleviate by sharing them, surely my pages cannot fail to do the only duty my regard requires. Intense interest in your welfare will dictate to my pen; and my best judgement shall endeavour to correct it. I shall begin what strong presentiment forewarns me must be one of the most important letters I can ever write you, with the expression of my regret, that your aunt should so decidedly disapprove your having settled in Paris for three, or, perhaps, four years to come. Her own objection, and that of 'the Thistlethwaytes, and all Jane's friends' seem passing in leisurely review before me; for you have taught me to respect their opinions; and, besides, it is in all cases, a fearful thing to run against so strong a stream of family wishes and advice, unless one course be urged by hard necessity or by some great expediency that Reason's self bears up against the tide. I think you have succeeded in proving to me a little of the one, and much of the other. Perhaps it is undoubted to English people, in general, that, where our circumstances are favorable, no country in the world furnishes better opportunities of sound education, than England: but there are gradations of education in England as elsewhere, from high to low, from very good to very indifferent; and the highest, and the best, are, too frequently, beyond the reach of those who might profit from them most. It is not much more than a year since I was making anxious inquiries on this subject for my friend, Miss McL(ean), and was interested in the decision of Mrs Best (Miss Norcliffe's sister) respecting the finishing of her two daughters, at that time thirteen and fifteen. The two latter are with Miss Shepherd of Brompton (Bromley?) whom I have before mentioned to you at, I believe, £300 a year each including everything, and considered a very moderate expense. Miss McLean's friend (the daughter of Mrs Grieve's) is to be continued in France a year longer, and then, when between sixteen and seventeen, to finish her studies and be introduced in Edinburgh, where her mother will settle. I have heard much of the education to be gained in Bath. The Norcliffes took their governess and were four winters there (during one of which I was with them) for the sake of masters. Sir John Astley (of Everley) sent his two daughters to the best school there. The Norcliffes learnt *solids* at home, *dancing* at Bath, and finish in society and abroad. I saw her a couple of years ago, seemed to me to be more in want of mentalities and manners, than, perhaps, a baronet's daughter of seventeen ought to be in this enlightened age. I know not much of Bath at present. Miss McLean tells me, I should not now like its style of society, for it is much altered: but Bath used not to be either a very literary place, or a very cheap one. Hulius, we all know, painted flowers very beautifully; but he charged half a guinea a lesson for teaching a rose bud per annum. Surely N -'s beautiful style of sketching was taught her by her master in the country; my first remembrance of the effect produced by the masters she had in Bath (in 1813) would persuade me, they were not altogether worth poor Jane's scolding music mistress, who makes her play nevertheless. It is observed by Gibbon that a man has two educations, one that is given to him, one that he gets himself. How far this may be the case with ladies, perhaps it might be more difficult to determine, but I have seen from very many examples that it is impossible for girls to have been at what are called the best schools in England, yet still, in spite of English grounding, know too many littles of everything to know much of anything. But to come still more closely to the point, let us consider what it is we want. That is, what constitutes what is esteemed a good education for any English gentlewoman, make comparisons as fairly as we can, Saturday 28 May. It will probably be allowed that the following are the items of a very liberal education — English, French and Italian, writing, arithmetic, geography, the use of the globes, history, music, drawing and dancing. I have seen the catalogue swelled by chronology, astronomy, natural philosophy, theology, &c. The first is, or ought to be comprehended in history; it is probable that enough of the second and third may be introduced with the study of the globes; and that the best part of the last is taught by parents who 'train up a child in the way he should go'. But with whatever advantages a young lady may pursue these studies in London, will it be disputed that with respect to all but England, she may have equal advantages in Paris. Is there not there, as in your own capital, a description of persons knowing, well enough for the instruction of young ladies, the rules of arithmetic — the real divisions of the earth, and the imaginary ones of the heavens, the deeds of men, and the fame, or infamy, of their natures? As for French, Italian, music, drawing, dancing, those fashionable, those almost necessary accomplishments of the day, which fire the eye of admiration and gather round them all the éclat of the world, are these worse taught, worse learnt in Paris, than in London? Why does Major Eliot send his daughters to Paris, after having given them the best masters in London? But let us examine Jane. Was she not nearly thirteen, when first trusted some few yards from her mother's apron-string at a school in Paris, of which one of the two ladies who keeps it is an Englishwoman? Had you sent Jane to any school in England, would she have made a greater improvement in any one thing she has learnt? I doubt it much. I doubt even that she would have known her own language more grammatically, or that she could have written a letter in better English than she can at present. A friend of mine[2], with the best masters in York, then celebrated, and justly celebrated, for its masters, could not write English correctly at fourteen; nor, with all their teaching, was she, as far as they were concerned, as clever as Jane.She had learnt music from the age of seven with some year or two's interruption, and could not play so well. Halfpenny[3], who published the architectural ornaments of York cathedral, was her drawing master, and she drew not much better, after her instructions, than she did at ten before having had any at all. She had learnt arithmetic from her youth up, and tortured many a poor slate with what they called mathematics, and problems geographical and astronomical, yet, left to herself, could not do a common compound division sum. She knew, in reality, scarce a word of French, though in the constant practice of dictating the exercises of all her class (remembering more happily than the rest what their master had said to them) and being, in fact, the Solomon of the school, she had written in a letter, at ten years old, of Themistocles and Antides. Her friends and all her pastors and masters were gulled alike, and she would have been to this day a choice example of 'English grounding' but for a something of better kind within, that worked its own way, and, in the next half dozen years, succeeded better. What *I* call grounding is perhaps not generally acquired at a girls' school, even in England. The young lady must learn like the rest, and then, if she will have her literary building *solid* must, like Gibbon, dig her foundation deeper, and throw in new materials of her own. But, surely, till we are strong enough to do for ourselves, a change of architects is bad. No two agree; and, perhaps, it is wiser to be content with uniform mediocrity, than shew a patchwork of incongruities where scattered beauty is but the glimmering that makes the darkness of perfection more visible. Putting expense out of the question, were Jane at once transplanted to the best school in London, what time would she require to learn new modes of learning, and unlearn all her old ones? From her own confession, it is but lately that she has learnt to learn in Paris. Send a boy from school to school, he is perpetually put back. Eton is good, and Westminster is good; it matters not which is the better. A boy may be made a scholar at either — only do not change him from the one to the other, but let him go on quietly where he began. If, however, the argument is to be shifted from 'English grounding' (as, I suspect, it is at heart) to 'she will be a complete French girl' this throws it off the hinge of literary acquirement, and hangs it on that of national prejudice. A Highland friend of mine will not have his daughter educated in the midst of good connections in London, for fear they should become too English: he will have them in Edinburgh, lest Highland feeling should degenerate in the capital of South Britain.

(Sunday 29 May). Were a girl of twelve or thirteen sent abroad for four or five years, and completely separated from all her family, it would be natural that her tastes and habits should assume the character of those with whom she was placed; but were she for ever under the watchful eye of a parent whom she was proud to imitate, and whose unyielding nationality stamped its own impression with that unperceived, yet mighty force, a mother's love, would not this mould the young mind, and fix its living form for ever? In such a case, surely religion could not be in danger; and all a mother's care would guard each avenue to that mysterious source within, whence issues, at affection's bidding, our future happiness or misery. If Jane has a heart, she will appreciate more and more the devoted tendings with which you have placed on her your every thought, and wish, and hope. She will mourn over the pangs and doubts that distracted you, and regard, and gratitude, and pride, will rouse her to repay them; amid the Éclat of French mannerism she will preserve the steadiness and the dignity of English principle, and, will prove to her friends that the elegant agrémens

---

2 Miss Lister is in reality referring to herself.

3 Joseph Halfpenny, (1748-1811), artist and engraver, helped with the restoration of York cathedral; he was the author of *Gothic ornaments in the Cathedral Church of York* (1800), and *Fragmenta Vetusta* (1807).

of the one country may, like a beautiful veil, but shew off more gracefully the solid worth of the other. But I have dwelt too long on this subject. I could have mentioned more families than one who find the plan of foreign education (under the parents' eye) answer — the Valvasours, Stainforths, &c., but you know them not — you have never heard me name them. The Stainforths returned a year or two ago. The girls (the oldest about thirteen when they went) after a four years' residence at Tours, and one year spent in travelling, are much admired; nor have I ever heard them spoken of by anyone as too French. At all rates, there is something in good French mannerism distingué, and à la mode, in the higher circles of English society, at present. For my own part, I must honestly confess between ourselves, the *dowdyism* of the people one sees afloat in London, is very striking after a seven months' sojourn in Paris. The Mackenzies made the same remark, and hoped they had not yet lost all trace of Parisian exterior. I have had a lecture from Miss Maclean for inadvertently observing that Mrs Grieves, elegant as she seems to have been from her very cradle, could never have looked so elegant had she not lived abroad. I was not aware of all this till my return home. I now feel that I am improved; yet, that I am nevertheless sufficiently proud of my country and thoroughly English and thoroughly Yorkshire at heart, none, surely, who has the smallest knowledge of me, would deny. But no more. I respect the opinion of your aunt, and have therefore written so much. Read it to her, if you like. She will not at all agree with me, and the barometer of my judgement will sink much, but I like not credit undeserved, and would rather live quietly in my own Lilliput, than stray beyond my sphere in the opinion of anyone . . . I can always read your writing quite well. Thank you for your *judgment* in correcting mine. In the dictionary I commonly use is written on the margin 'Judgement — Walker'. I remember long since adopting this spelling in consequence of the observation that the e was inserted to prevent the meeting of the consonants and for the more visible softening of the g; but, being now older and, I trust, wiser than I was some years ago — less curious of 'verbal singularities', and less apt to forget that 'words are the daughters of earth, and that things are the sons of heaven', I shall return to the judgment of the generality, and be glad to save a letter where I can. Have you not found me write abridgment, acknowledgment and all such words with the supernumerary e? I like your criticisms exceedingly.

Letter from Anne Lister at Shibden Hall to Sibbella Maclean of Coll, at Tobermory, 19 October 1825.

... Miss Pickford is daughter to the late Sir Joseph Radcliffe, made a baronet on account of his useful and spirited exertions as a magistrate in the time of the Luddites (those hereabouts precursors of the radicals), and is aunt to the present Sir Joseph who married a Miss Macdonald of Berwick. By the way, do you know anything about her? She is a Roman Catholic. As a lady, Miss P(ickford) is the most learned person I have ever met with; and, perhaps, she is as amiable, as human nature may permit. One cannot exactly say, she has all sorts of sense but common sense, because she is an excellent woman of business; but she is very eccentric — of her sisters, one chose to marry a vulgar attorney in Halifax (who died some time ago) .... Perhaps we none of us very well know ourselves; but I am as generally, and as equally cheerful and happy as most people I meet with, and am really and truly seldom more than five minutes in reconciling myself to whatever disagreeables may beset me. Do turn to my letter again. Perhaps it is merely in that dry sort of style that you would better understand if you had passed a winter with me at Shibden. I have sometimes, they tell me, a way of saying things peculiarly my own. I smiled to read, that it would not now surprise you 'so much', even if I should marry. Be prepared for all things; for I am persuaded 'joy flies monopolists'; and, if you are '*one*', and I am not another 'made to live alone'. I could be happy in a *garret*, or a cellar with the object of my regard; but, in solitude, a prison or a palace would be all alike to me. 'Did Mrs B(arlow) ask your opinion as to marrying?' No! but knowing the circumstances, I have ventured to give it. I have ventured to urge, that the rational union of two amiable persons must be productive of comfort. Trust me, Sibbella, however much you may fancy you differ with me on this subject, we are at heart agreed. There is no pleasure like that of thought meeting thought 'ere from the lips it part'. Give me a mind in unison with my own, and I'll find the way of happiness — without it, I should feel alone among multitudes; and all the world would seem to me a desert. I was sorry to find it possible for any party of travellers to give such

87

an account of Lady E. B(utler)[4] and Miss Ponsonby. The latter is several years (ten I think) younger than the former, and must be four or five or more years less than eighty. Her first appearance struck me as much, and perhaps, as unfavorably as possible; but there was a flash of mind that bore down on all; and I shall never forget the enchantment that it threw on all around. Lady E. B(utler) I have never seen. She was once clever. What she is, it might be humiliating to inquire; for, in this world, minds, like bodies, do appear to wear out. About the time I was at Llangollen[5] the difficulty of seeing the ladies (any one might see the place) seemed considerable. I regret that it is lessened, but the burden of age may lessen the quantity of self-derived resources and thus aggravate the necessity of picking up amusement wherever it is to be had. Lady E. B(utler) has been quite blind more than a year. She had always high spirits, and was always, in this respect, a contrast to her graver friend whom I can well enough imagine to consenting to admit strangers for her friend's sake, and sitting, scarcely uttering a word, intently and almost unconsciously gazing on the eye that could behold that gaze no more. Changed indeed must she be, if there be not a spirit still within her, that, if one spark had lighted it, could not have beamed with all the light of noonday life and intellect! But no more. Should we decay as these have done, may there at last, remain some proud and haughty feelings of reserve, that bars us from the stare of strangers! I did not at all care about not being able to go to the last festival. Had Mr Salmon, or Madame Pasta sung, I might have had some wish about it; as it was, Mrs L(awton) and I thought ourselves quite as happy where we were, as we could have been either in the cathedral, or half squeezed to death at the fancy-ball in the new concert-room ... But do try your utmost to let us have an opportunity of coming to a fair understanding of each other's dispositions, &c., &c., next spring. I shall not dare to think much

---

[4] Lady Eleanor Butler (1745-1829), recluse of Llangollen. About 1774 she and a friend, Sarah Ponsonby, decided to live in complete isolation from society. This they did for about fifty years, and by their eccentricities were known as 'the ladies of the vale', and were often visited by tourists.

[5] July 1822.

of it for fear of disappointment; but a fortnight will be infinitely better than nothing; and I would endeavour to return with you, if possible. Surely, *I shall know you* some time.

Friday morning, 4 November .... I have persuaded my uncle to let me cut down all the fine fir and larch timber planted by one of my great uncles about sixty years ago. We have had a great deal of pruning, planting, fencing; and I cannot get these things done to my mind without looking after them myself. I hope to be quiet by and by, tho' while circumstanced as I am at present, perhaps the hope is more pleasing than true. I perpetually think of you and your 'Yorkshire road-maker', and treasure up your observations on this subject like gold. Thank you — thank you. You are ever kind, candid, and judicious. You are the only one who has reminded me not to deteriorate myself in endeavouring to improve our place. You have done me more good and I am more sincerely obliged to you than you think. Oh! that it were possible for you to come here! You would do me still greater good. I think you would be happy, and that I should not much disappoint you in anything. I dare not just now talk of going to you next summer. This appalling loss of the *Comet*[6] has frightened my uncle and aunt. 'You might have been on board, and then — Oh! stay at home — stay at home.' I sat an hour and a half with Miss Pickford yesterday. She is come to her sister for ten days. She told me, Sir Joseph and Lady Radcliffe would have been on board themselves along with their six unfortunate servants, but the packet was not large enough to take their carriages. What a providential escape! ... Your history of the poor girl to whom you have been so kind and so judiciously merciful interested me exceedingly. What matter it what may be said by those reputed 'righteous' — those often pharisees of their day who leave the exercise of their charity to those samaritans whom in their ignorance they despise? I hope and trust, Sibbella, that, had I been in your place, I should have done as you have done. What did our Saviour with the woman taken in adultery? Come to Shibden, my good friend, bring the poor man's letter with you, let us read it together, and perhaps you will find that our opinions on all material subjects are

---

[6] *The Comet* was the first steam-boat on the Clyde, launched in 1812.

sufficiently agreed. You will have no difficulty in making my friends yours. You will have no 'wonder' to encounter from my uncle and aunt. Common justice will prevent their wondering at my choice, and regard for me will prevent their wondering at yours. You may talk of 'shyness' at a distance, but you will forget it all when you come. You will find my uncle and aunt all kindness, and myself in affection, at least, all that I have ever professed. I shall never change towards you at heart, here, or in Paris, of wherever else I may be. The place you occupy in my regard is safe against time, absence, *matrimony*, or whatever other circumstance may occur; and I do profess, and do believe myself to be now and for ever, Sibbella, your very affectionate and very faithful friend,

A.L. -

Draft letter from Anne Lister at Shibden Hall to Mrs Maria Barlow in Paris, 3 December 1825.

... I suppose it is the Mr Duncombe who was there (William oldest son of the present Charles D(uncombe) of Duncombe Park) that our county is now soliciting to come forward with Mrs Norcliffe's cousin, Mr Fountaque Wilson, to be our two anti-catholic members in the next parliament. After much discussion, some time back, of the disfranchisement of the borough of Grampound in Cornwall, the right of electing the additional members was given to our county, and we are all on the alert. Six candidates will offer themselves. Our present members, Lord Milton and Mr Stuart Wortley, Lord Morpeth and Mr Bethel for the catholic emancipation; Mr Wilson and Mr Duncombe against it. The tide of popular feeling is strong; and the two last are almost sure to be elected. But we are harassed just now. All Great Britain is harassed about the stability of our provincial banks, of which we are said to have altogether about seven hundred. Seven have just stopt payment within twenty miles of us. It is impossible as yet to calculate the loss. Public confidence is shaken. 'Tis said, in the panic of the moment hardly a third of them will be able to stand, but our two at Halifax will be among the number. Our funds are low — three per cent consuls at eighty-three and a fraction more than ten per cent lower than some months back. But things are expected to amend in the spring. In spite of all, great public improvements are going on in all directions; and there is no apparent want of money. I envy you your fine weather. On writing my first page we were enveloped in snow. For the last ten days we have had nothing but thick fog and rain — the ground saturated with water. The cholera morbus which has been fatal hereabouts, is wearing itself out; but everybody is suffering from rheumatism, colds, swelled faces, or something or other. My aunt can hardly stir. My uncle is very asthmatic. I still live out of doors . . . Thank you for your recipe for chapt hands. Tell Jane, with my love, her remedy, however good in the Tuileries Gardens, would be absolutely impossible in the woods at Shibden . . .

8

ADVENTURES IN SWITZERLAND; THE TYROL AND ITALY

1826-1827

The death of James Lister at Shibden Hall occurred in January 1826, and after settling his affairs, Anne Lister and her aunt decided to make a prolonged stay on the continent, mainly for the sake of the elder Miss Lister's health. The majority of the letters of this period related to their travelling experiences.

Draft letter from Anne Lister at Shibden Hall to Mrs Maria Barlow in Paris.

Shibden. Friday night. 27 January 1826.

Maria! My uncle is no more! We thought not of danger — he seemed not to think of it himself as if it was so near. The shock was awfully sudden and unexpected. His medical man considered him going on well, (he has, for the last month past, suffered considerably from difficulty of respiration), and talked of nothing but recovery. He got up yesterday morning, as usual, about nine, and, in the act of dressing, fell down, and, from the rupture of some large blood vessel near the heart, expired instantaneously. My poor aunt is as well as can be expected. God bless you, Maria!

Shibden. Tuesday afternoon. 21 February 1826.

Maria! Excuse my writing on thicker paper than usual. I am in a hurry, and have not time (the stock in my writing box being done) to seek for the few remaining sheets I have of very thin paper. I wish my letter to go by tomorrow's post, or you cannot get it these ten days ... My aunt's plans are not decided as yet, she is too unwell, but she is strongly advised to spend next winter in the south of France, or at Nice. Bordeaux and Toulouse are recommended if we think Nice too distant. Do give my love to Mme Droz,[1] and ask her to tell you, if we can be comfortably accommodated in Bordeaux, and what sort of society we can have there. We shall be a party of four — our two selves, and a man, and a maid. Some say, 'Take your own carriage'. Some say not. I saw no travelling carriage in Paris, equal to my own. Do let me have your opinion ... I am sorry Mme Droz has failed to you in another of her promises — this is not the English part of her character. You do me much good by naming all these things so candidly. Without placing much reliance on her, do ask her what introductions she would be good enough to give me to her friends in Bordeaux. Tell her, with my love, I have particularly desired you to say, she needs have no fear I shall alarm them, as I did her at Battle, with strong boots — that we shall live according to the rules of English comfort, with no thought of doing dishonour to ourselves, or our country. I am not sorry our friend has so many correspondents. I have no time for writing letters which are not either of necessity, or of the deepest interest to my heart. I have much to think of, and to do. My uncle's confidence and affection have placed me in a very responsible and by no means unoccupying situation. The executorship is left solely to me; and it is not one of the least possible trouble. I shall be obliged to look over the whole of my uncle's papers, and rearrange them and it will be some weeks before we can get quit of the workmen. We shall leave here as soon as possible — perhaps in May. My father and sister take our place, and we theirs, till we can let the house they now occupy, and be off altogether. The declining state of my aunt's health is a subject of deep anxiety to me. I hope she will rally; but I dare not calculate on her return to strong health ... I think you are right to have Jane vaccinated. Tell me how she goes on in her studies ... Can you, without trouble, get to know the price of posting in France, and what one ought to pay the postboys; for all my friends give different accounts; and some

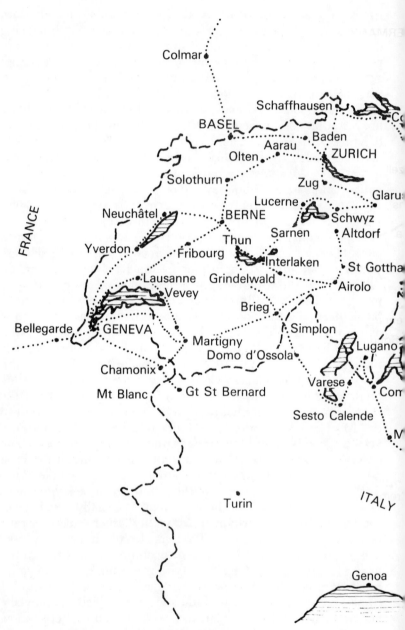

Anne Lister's route through Switzerland and the Tyrol
to Venice 1827

94

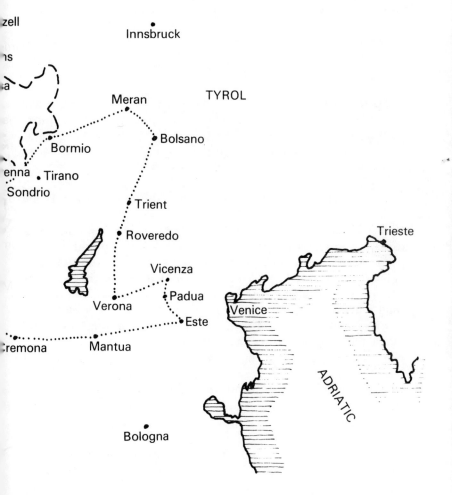

of them must have been egregiously cheated. What ought one to pay for veturino[2] horses from Calais to Paris, and from Bordeaux, or Toulouse, or Nice, or Marseilles? What distance can one travel veturino per day, and how much should one pay per day? Tell me all this, if you can conveniently; but do not give yourself any trouble about it. I am writing in a great hurry. Excuse me — think only of the heart that dictates, and of the perfect esteem, and faithful attachment that will ever be felt towards you by your affectionately devoted,

A.L. -

A Madame
  Made Barlow
    Quai Voltaire No 15 à Paris.

From June to October 1827 Miss Lister travelled with her friend Mrs Maria Barlow and the latter's young daughter, Jane, in Switzerland and Italy. The following letters which passed between Miss Lister and her aunt, whom she had left in Paris, describe the different stages of the journey.

Three Kings Hotel, Basle. Monday 25 June 1827.

You will easily believe, my dear aunt, that I have not had much time for letter-writing before now. I have thought of you perpetually, and longed to know how you were going on; but I have not been uneasy. I have persuaded myself that you are comfortable, that the fine weather does you good, and that I shall find you, on my return, considerably better than I left you. For my own part, I feel the good of this rummage; and, now that I have made up for lost rest, am well. George would tell you how we got off from home. We had delightful weather, and reached Nancy about five on Sunday morning, the 17th inst. They were going to celebrate the *fête dieu*; and, as soon as we

---

[1] Wife of M. le Capitaine Droz, French littérateur, and a Paris friend of Anne Lister.

[2] Hired carriage horses.

had breakfasted, and made ourselves decent, off we were to the grand military mass at the cathedral, whence the procession set off. An untravelled English person can hardly imagine such an absurd piece of mummery in these days. The people have ceased to go down upon their knees as formerly; and the host is taken up, and set down again, without anybody's seeming to care much about it. We then went up and down to see all the lions. The public buildings are very handsome, and Nancy is justly esteemed one of the handsomest cities in France. I longed to have written to you tho' but a few lines; but, after being up two nights, and being obliged to be off at six the next morning (Monday 18th), I felt, I ought to have as much bed as I could, hurried over some boiled milk and strawberries, and was asleep before eight. We entered Strasbourg at five fifteen, on Tuesday morning (the 19th), and here, after breakfasting, settled about our passports, and walking about a little to stretch my legs, was glad to get into bed about noon, and sleep till between four and five the next morning. Wednesday (the 20th) we went to the very top of the spire (just under the couronne, or ball, which is merely five steps higher — I was not, at the time, aware of this), a giddy height of 490 feet by 658 steps! The last 158 steps are really tremendous. The tread is about fourteen inches by four in the broadest part, the rise of each step being full nine inches. But what chiefly constitutes the tremendous is, that, except the staircase, this part of the tower is completely a piece of open work, there being all the way, and all round, open gothic window-frames about nine feet high by nearly half as much broad, having no guard but a single small bar of iron across the middle. If you look down for a moment, it must be along the newel of the staircase, or thro' the window-frames upon the country below, a sight more terribly sublime than any I have yet beheld. When at the top, and sufficiently settled to look about you, the view is magnificent — worth all the trouble — the Rhine, the mountains of France and Germany. On the third day of August 1737, an earthquake made this hujus tower rock like a cradle, for ten minutes. During the heat of summer, it attracts the electric fluid. Damage is often done; and the man told us, they had generally storms about twice a week. Fancy the two west towers of York minster — on the top of that on the south side, the man has his house (one story high, very comfortable), the flat roof over the space of nave between the towers forming a sort of court — then at the top of the other tower, is the cloak-room, and one or two more little rooms, and over them rises this tremendous steeple, looking so light and open, that it seems but like gothic tracery. I thought of you, and bought a good print of the cathedral for you to look at on my return. We next saw the famous monument of Marshall Saxe, in St Thomas's church, the theatre, &c. Thursday 21st we crossed the famous quarter-of-a-mile-long bridge of boats over the Rhine, and sat an hour in a German cottage at the picturesque extremity of the town of Kehl, where we had sourish cream and German bread. The Rhine at Kehl is a magnificent river — its waters were turbid from the great quantity of rain that had fallen in the mountains; its current rapid as in Caesar's time. In returning two officers of the 9th French Infantry shewed us over the citadel, and we afterwards went to the museum, botanic garden, &c. At eleven on Friday morning (the 22nd) left Strasbourg for Basle — reached Colmar at six — saw the very pretty cathedral (the neatest, cleanest Roman Catholic place of worship I have ever seen out of England), dined at eight — left Colmar at nine fifteen, and reached Basle about half past seven on Saturday morning (23rd inst.). The fertile plain of Alsace is magnificently bounded by the Vosges, and the Schwartzwald, or black mountains of Germany. Not one peep of the Rhine, tho' so near to it all along, except for a little while, about five miles before reaching Sierentz. The river is completely embosomed in wood. The Vosges mountains repeatedly reminded me of Blackstonedge, only that their acclivities and summits are often beautifully wooded. On reaching Basle, we had a thousand things to do — to unpack, and send linen to the wash, &c., &c. I was obliged to have my hair cut, an operation of two full hours. At the table d'hôte we met the famous Saxon botanist and Councillor of State M. Bridell de Brideric[3] a very gentlemanly man about fifty. He took us to the botanic garden here, and introduced us to the professor — to the public library, and introduced us to the learned mathematical professor Hubert, and then went with us to the cathedral. I was too much tired to be able to do more than write out the notes of my journal, and go to bed. Yesterday (the 24th) settled accounts, &c., &c., went to the cathedral — a mixture of Saxon and early gothic, and very interesting. Walked along the ramparts, and about the town — dined at half past eight, (the table d'hôte supper hour), and went to bed as soon as I could. This morning (25th inst.), is really the first opportunity I have had of writing. Never was more comfortable at any Inn in my life. My room is on two sides surrounded by the Rhine. We are a little way from the wooden bridge that connects the great and little Basle — the two skirt along the river's banks, the line of white houses beautifully broken here and there by poplars and other trees. The view is magnificent, bounded by the mountains of the black forest, and by the wooded range of Jura. I shall keep the rest of my paper to tell you our future route. I fear I shall not be able to write you many such letters as this. What with going about, keeping my journal, and accounts, I have enough to do. But I know you will take the will for the deed, and be satisfied merely to know that I am well.

Tuesday night 26 June 1827. I expected a letter from Mariana, but it is not come. I shall inquire again tomorrow morning. However, the man has very civilly promised to forward her pages immediately. I shall not make myself uneasy either about you or her but shall always go on hoping for the best. We are to be off at eight in the morning for the lesser falls of the Rhine at Lauffenburgh, where we shall sleep. Thursday we hope to sleep at Baden, see the baths, &c., &c., and get to Zurich on Friday night or Saturday, where we talk of staying a couple of days, and then proceeding to Schaffhausen, thence to Constance — beyond this, we are not at present, quite determined. We must see how our time goes on. However, we shall certainly make for Berne by some longer or shorter route; for our *voiturier* (coachman) is from there. We agreed with him yesterday, tried him today to the Chateau and gardens of Arlesheim, and like him, and his carriage (a *calêche*, with a gig-top for half the carriage and leathers that will cover in all the rest if required) and horses very well. We shall thus, in this respect, be very comfortable for a napoleon a day. The greatest plague is the money, perpetually varying in superscription and value, and always tiresome to a degree you cannot easily imagine. We make a point of dining at the table d'hôte, because

---

[3] Baron Samuel Elisée Bridel (later Samuel Elias von Bridel Brideri), 1761-1828. Swiss naturalist and poet. He published some botanical works and was secretary to the Prince of Saxe-Gotha.

we always meet with very respectable, pleasant people who are perpetually of use to us. A German party went with us today to Arlesheim. We are well satisfied to have entered Switzerland via Basle, we come so well, and gradually upon its beauties. Everything has gone well with us so far. Till the 15th of next month, direct to me poste restante, à Berne, Suisse — afterwards, post restante à Genève, Suisse. I shall give the same direction to Mariana. Respecting the journey, I have written her nearly a verbatim copy of what I have written to you. I hope you will get this letter on Sunday morning, and that you will not have thought me too long in sending it off. Travelling four days and four nights in one week makes one require a little rest. We have all borne our journey marvellously well. We shall now have no more night-work, till our return home per diligence. In Switzerland we can order our carriage when we like, and suit ourselves. Should you write to Shibden, do give my best love to my father and Marian. At present, I must not write more. I ought to be in bed, and shall only add, that I am always, my dear aunt, very affectionately yours,

A.L. -

Mrs and Miss B(arlow) desired me not to forget to give their best remembrances, and to tell you, they are delighted with Switzerland.

Constance. Monday 2 July 1827.

You will easily believe, my dear aunt, that we are too much taken up with sight-seeing to have many moments to spare. Even in the carriage we are reading descriptions of our routes, or making short notes, or, very occasionally overcome with the excessive heat in the valleys, taking a few minutes nap — but we do not slumber long; for the country is everywhere so beautiful and interesting, we keep awake in spite of ourselves. I am very much better for my journey. Proximity to the Rhine which disagreed with us all, made us all ill at first, seems now to have done me good. In fact, whether we had been inclined or not, we should have been driven out of Basle. You can have no idea of the strong smell there is from the water, almost as if of sea-weed. This produced, for the time, the most violent bowel complaint I ever remember to have had. But I am better for it now. I finished my last in such a hurry, I know not whether I mentioned this or not. At all rates, I was perfectly well of the moment we had got out of Basle. However, in nearing the Rhine afterwards, we all felt a little sickish again — but this was all. We left Basle on Wednesday morning, the 27th ult., went to Lauffenburgh, were much interested with the little falls, stood near an hour over the very spot where twenty-nine? years ago Lord Montague and Mr Burdett were engulphed, watching the timber as it floated down the rapids to be embarked below, and then went to the pretty little town of Frik where we slept. Thursday the 28th ult., we reconnoitred the old castle of Habsbourg, the cradle of the house of Austria, dined with about (upwards of) sixty people at the table d'hôte at the baths of Schinznach (like Harrogate water — the ex-queen of Holland there), saw the interesting old abbey of Konigsfelden, and crossed the Reuss by the bridge of the beautiful little village of Windisch (the Vindonissa of the Romans). From the top of the hill is a fine view of the confluence of the Aar, Reuss, and Limmat. From Windisch to Baden the drive is perfectly beautiful. On leaving the other two rivers, we had the Limmat, whose high, beautifully sloping right bank is one continued vineyard. On getting to the gate of Baden, we turned down to the left, to the great Baths, a village romantically situated on the left bank of the Limmat. Friday evening, 6 July 1827. Crown Hotel at Rorshach, on the lake of Constance. Since Monday, my dear aunt, I have really had no time for getting on with my letter, and have been obliged to be contented with thinking of, instead of writing to you. I am for ever musing how you are going on, and hoping you are better and better. However, as I know you will wish to know what we have been about, I shall proceed with the sketch of our journey. We were very comfortable at Baden. From my bedroom, I went down a back staircase to my bath, lined with wood, about twenty-seven yards square and a yard deep. The natural heat of the water thirty-two Reamur, cooled down to twenty-eight, was so equal, so luxurious, I could have staid in three hours, instead of three quarters of an hour — the water of the same kind as that at Schinznach, but tasted milder, and had no bad smell. The country about Baden very beautiful, delightful walks — we were sorry to be off so soon. Friday 29th ult., off from Baden — beautiful drive, and got to Zurich in three hours, a little before one. Just in time for the table d'hôte — went in hot, and covered with dust — who should chance to be my neighbour but the Revd Mr Robt Swann of York,[4] whom you remember a little boy at Scarbro'. He was to be off at three and we were going to see the town. He said he should not be at home of three months — was gong to return by way of Germany — had his servant and carriage and three horses with him. We had all of us heard so much of the beauty of Zurich, that, already spoilt by beauty elsewhere, we were almost disappointed. Yet the lake is beautiful, and the town finely placed at the head of it. Meaning to see more of the lake on our return from the Grisons, and afraid to miss seeing the falls of the Rhine at the best time, we went to Schaffhausen on Saturday the 30th ult., and had the good fortune to see the fall in perfection that evening. The prints represent them very fairly. At the first peep, without being exactly disappointed, I caught myself saying, 'Well, I suppose, I shall never be astonished with any falls unless I should see those of Niagara'. However, on crossing the river (a little distance below the falls) to the château of Lauffen, contemplating them from the giddy height, and then descending to the little wooden bridge that juts almost into the very foam of the fall, the horrible sublime of the latter situation made me sensible that it was worth while to travel all the way from Paris, merely to see the falls of the Rhine. They were four hundred and two feet broad and there were sixty-eight feet of fall, the greatest depth, within half a foot, attained this year, after such a winter of snow. The view I like best is from the village side (village of Lauffen) just before entering the village. The banks of the Rhine are magnificent; and the immediate scenery is worthy of the falls. It is by quietly contemplating them for some time, that one understands how they deserve to be so celebrated. When the melting of the snow on the mountains subsides, the river is so low, the peasants ford it just above the falls, and dine upon the rock in the midst of them. We longed for the same good fortune we had had at the little falls, at Lauffenburgh, to see huge trees floated down, one of which was literally whirled on end, and stood upright for a second or two. Slept at Schaffhouse (or spelt Schaffhausen) on the 30th ult., and proceeded to Constance on Sunday the 1st instant. Monday and Tuesday (the 2nd and 3rd inst.) went about Constance, and the environs, the isle of Meinau in the lake, &c., &c. A nice town — the lake *beautiful* — the surrounding mountains not lofty enough to make its pretensions of a higher order. Wednesday the 4th inst., strolled over the convent of Münsterlingen, drank some excellent wine in the cellar, (the long vaulted cellars full of huge casks that hold 5 or 6,000 bottles, are worth seeing), and shook hands with the lady abbess. Skirted the lake for about three hours, then mounted the hills (magnificent views of the lake) to the beautiful and romantically situated little town of St Gall. The abbey church is the most beautiful Grecian (Corinthian) church we have ever seen. The view from the top of the Frendenberg (immediately above the town of St Gall) is magnificent. In fact we admire St Gall exceedingly. Thursday 5th inst. from St Gall to Gais, a very pretty village among the mountains, where people go to *drink milk*, and bathe — dined at the table d'hôte with about thirty people. After dinner, went to Appenzell romantically situated, but the people Roman Catholic, poor, and almost all beggars. Nothing looked decent but the church; and this was quite spruce with painted ceilings, &c., &c. There did not seem to be an inn where we could hope to be comfortable — we, therefore, made the best of our way, up and down mountain after mountain (very fine scenery — peeps at the high snow-streaked every now and then), to Trogen, where we slept last night. Such hills and such roads, you have only seen in the vale of Festiniog, down upon Tan y Bwlch. The scenery is quite indescribable — hills, valleys, woods, rocks, rivers, villages — white wooden cottages sprinkled over the fresh green pastures, and fantastically thrown together among high mountains half hidden by clouds. Left Trogen for Rheinek, to see the junction of the Rhine with the Lake of Constance, and then came here (two leagues farther) to see this lively little capital of the lake, a pretty village — the emporium for corn from Suabia, and for all the traffic of the lake. We meant to have come from Rheinek by water, but the lake was too rough — 'tis literally like a sea — the waves splashed against the carriage as we drove along. The road from Trogen to Rheinek is so mountainous, we walked five miles out of the nine, the ascents and descents being really tremendous — but, literally, our eyes are always more tired than our legs. The scene changed almost at every step, that our *visionary* powers have, absolutely, no rest. For the last few days, we have been completely among the German-Swiss, and are thankful to meet anyone who speaks French. Our present aubergiste is Italian; and it is quite new

103

to us to have to *hack* at Italian. The people seem to meet together, all hereabouts, to sing, in an evening, and really sing, all in concert, very well. They sing, or gurgle the Tyrolese air. If you can imagine this beautiful air sung in a *beautiful vox-humana, turkey-cock-splutter*, perhaps you can have some idea of the Tyrolese air as executed by the throat of a German-Swiss peasant. Quite little boys and girls do it alike well. Today has been coolish and pleasant; but we have had some very hot weather — suffocatingly hot in the woods in the bottoms of the valleys. At three yesterday afternoon, the thermometer, lying on the carriage seat, stood at 98° and we have had it much warmer — (I mean in the sun). Fortunately for us, there has often been rain during the nights. We had a storm of thunder and lightning at Constance on Tuesday afternoon; and we have just had some refreshing rain here. We are to be off at six in the morning, to pursue our journey along the Rheintal (valley of the Rhine) to Coire, or, as the Germans call it, Chur. I shall keep my letter a few days, in the hope of telling you what we fix on there. (Vine-clad hills all along the Rhine — the high banks both of the Rhine, Reuss, and Limmat, as far as we have seen them, a continued vineyard.)

Coire, Tuesday morning, 10 July. I have got up at three o'clock to write you a few lines before we set off. From Rorshach (on Saturday the 7th inst.) we went direct to Sargans, one of the most finely mountain-seated little towns we ever saw. The whole of the Rheintal is fine; but from Oberried (not quite half way between Rorshach and Sargans) to here, it is magnificent. At the very picturesque little village of Trubbach (about three miles from Sargans) you suddenly come upon the rapid Rhine — the road winds for some distance along its brink, in places cut out of the rock that seems to rise 300 or 400 feet perpendicularly close above you on the right. On the left, at a little distance (for the valley is narrow) rise mountains not inferior in height. You can hardly imagine the magnificence of the scene, perpetually varying, yet not decreasing. We were very comfortable at Sargans, and should have staid there a day, had we had time to spare. On Sunday (the 8th inst.) the mountains still as magnificent as ever to the little town of Ragatz. From

---

[4] Robert Swann, M.A., Rector of Brandsby (1823), and Burton-Cherry; died 1872.

here we were to go to the celebrated baths of Pfaffers, and were on the tiptoe of expectation. The frightful gorge leading to the source of these baths, is (said to be) unique in Europe. You would have laughed to see us mounted. Such horses! such saddles! We had a guide at each horse's head — not more than needful. I could not have believed that *horses* could climb such a road — in many places about a yard wide — steep, wooded rock on one side; a frightful precipice down to the foaming Tamina on the other. We passed thro' the village of Valens, and, having ridden an hour and a quarter, could ride no farther. The mountain so steep, that, tho' the path was cut in traverses, it was almost impossible to walk steadily down it. After walking twenty-five minutes, came down upon the baths — the valley, at the foot of mountains which are, surely, seven or eight hundred feet high, almost perpendicular on each side — just broad enough for the narrow river and the line of buildings capable of accommodating two or three hundred persons, high and low, well packed above and below. No flat ground above the baths — the bare rock behind appears quite perpendicular — the wooded mountain — in front, so steep, it is cut in two or three terraces of perhaps seventy or eighty yards long (or not so much) that the invalids may have a little walk. Imagine this scene if you can. In the long passages within the building, are shops, as you have seen in the Palais de Justice at Paris. The table d'hôte was just over when we got there. About two hundred people there. But all was nothing to the frightful passage to the source — ten minutes' walk thro' this frightful gorge or cavern, over a couple of planks (very occasionally three planks in breadth), without any guard on the side next the water, wet and slippery with the dropping from the rock — deep below the foaming rapids of the Tamina: above a lofty cabin (high as the highest part of Castleton cavern), freshly lighted by two or three little breaks in of light from above — one false step, and you are lost. Never in my life did I see anything of the kind so appallingly fine. Returned to Ragatz in the evening. Yesterday (Monday the 9th inst.), we arrived here, a good town for Switzerland. Today, immediately, we are off for the Splugen, thence to Chiavenna, and the Italian lakes. You shall have my letter after we have crossed the mountain — from Chiavenna or Como. We shall reach the former tomorrow evening.

Verona, Saturday 21 July, 1827. You will wonder why I have

kept my pages so long by me. I feared their being lost, and determined to wait our arrival where safety might compensate for the delay. But, my dear aunt, I have no room to spare, and must bring up the account of our journey. On Tuesday the 10th inst., from Coire to Splugen, the celebrated Via Mala having even surpassed our expectations. Rested at Splugen, among the snow-mountains, on the 11th, glad to make up for lost sleep, and to set straight my journal and accounts. On Thursday the 12th, between walls of snow twelve or fifteen feet high, crossed the Splugen mountain (the much-talked-of new road into Italy, begun, as well as that over the St Bernardino, in 1819, and finished in 1825), and descended by one of the most frightfully magnificent roads in Europe into the fine valley of Chiavenna. A perfect vineyard; had we been a fortnight later, we should have had grapes. As it was, we had delicious figs, apricots, pears, gooseberries, cherries. Friday the 13th saw the lions of Chiavenna. Our guide a very civil man who had been eight years in England, lastly with Zanatti the print seller at Manchester. Saturday the 14th embarked on the Lake of Como for Domaso (lovely lake) — dined at Domaso, then crossed over to Colico where the carriage waited to take us to sleep at Morbegno in the Valteline. Sunday the 15th, our Italian friend (whom we had met yesterday on the lake, the head finance-inspector of the district, very civil and very useful) went with us as far as Sondrio (the capital of the Valteline, a fine wine-clad valley said to be one of the finest and most fertile in Europe); and we thence proceeded to Bormio to sleep. Monday the 16th, commenced our ascent to the famous three or four years ago completed pass into the Tirol over Monte Brauglio. A storm of thunder and lightning obliged us to sleep at the 5th station-house up the mountain (at the top of the Spondalunga) — here I had the ill-luck to find my thermometer broken; but the mountain-tops above us were covered with snow; and Mrs and Miss B(arlow) were half frozen to death. Not even eggs to be had. Tuesday the 17th, having wound up, as they said, on the whole forty-two traverses, got to the top of Monte Brauglio in an hour from where we slept. The road only just practicable thro' the snow — the look down from the top into the deep valley, or gorge below, the most terrific thing we ever saw. The snow had borne down all the railing; and the eye was appalled as it glanced down the forty-eight traverses (about ten feet wide) perfectly without guard, down the precipitous side of this huge mountain. The rains, the preceding night, had in places, washed down rubbish which the workmen were clearing away, but which still took up half the breadth of the road in two or three places. Even our coachman had begged us to get out at the top; and we walked down all the worst part of the way. The descent from Splugen was in some parts terrific; but there were woods, green pastures, white-washed villages, and scattered cottages, and beauty everywhere — here not a tree, nor a spot of green, nor cottage to be seen — huge peaks covered with snow — bare rugged rock-debris, and impending masses threatening destruction all around — the torrent not beautifully winding as from Splugen, but rushing straight along, and, narrow as it was, filling up the whole flat space between the mountains at the bottom. We were an hour from the top before we began to feel warm, and were not sorry to find ourselves at the little village of Prad, in the Tirol, at about ten a.m. From Prad to Meran, a good town, to sleep. Wednesday 18th from Meran thro' Bolsano, a good town, to Neumarkt (a poor place) to sleep. Thursday 19th from Neumarkt to Roveredo (a capital inn) to sleep. Friday 20th from Roveredo to Verona — we liked the Tirol exceedingly — the valleys are magnificent. At Bolsano we *seemed* to enter Italy, tho' Borghetto (about half way between Roveredo and here, Verona) is, in fact, the last town, or, rather, village in the Tirol. The valley from Bolsano to Verona is, literally, a garden of vines and mulberry trees, the Adige finely winding thro' the midst. Monday morning 23 July, 1827. After writing to you on Saturday, went to see the lions of the town. Yesterday went to the Lago di Gardo, very beautiful, but I prefer the Lake of Como. However, I was exceedingly interested yesterday at the ruins of the villa of Catullus, on the promontory of Sirmio. It juts beautifully into the lake, and is a lovely situation. It now belongs to a multitude of little land-owners — the remains of the villa are considerable, or, at least, there are several Roman arcades, two vaulted passages said to have led to the baths, and an oblong room (cellar) shewn as the bath-room. The day was lovely (we set off at five in the morning); the lake, at first too rough to venture upon, was smooth as glass as we watched its deep-blue waters murmur round the olive-clad Sirmio. We did not get back here (Verona) till seven thirty in the evening. It is a very interesting town. It would be worth while to come the whole way, were there nothing else to see than the amphitheatre, the most perfect Roman remain in the world. The Inn is excellent — we have a fine, lofty suite of three rooms, drawing room and two bedrooms. Excellent fruit, and very good cooking — we have pears, cherries, peaches, figs, and yesterday, had *grapes*; yet they say, the season is very late this year. The best months for Italy, are May, September and October — but, being so near, we could not resist taking a peep. The heat is certainly great; but the air is so dry and light, one is not oppressed as in England. Our eyes will close a little in the middle of the day; but our lungs can play freely; and respiration is easy. We are in a perpetual perspiration, but do not feel weakened by it. As we shall be ten days longer in Italy, we mean to travel in the night, from two to noon. Today we shall be off at four p.m., as this will give us plenty of time to get to Vicenza, between ten and eleven, to sleep. Thence by Padua to Venice, where we propose staying two whole days, and returning by Este, Mantua, Cremona, Lodi, Milan, Como, the Lake of Lugano, and the Lago Maggiore to Switzerland — whether by the St Bernardino, or by the Simplon, will depend upon the time we have left. From what place I shall write to you next I know not. We get over too much ground to have many leisure moments. Respecting the journey, I write exactly the same to you and Mariana. I have told her I fear you are a little dull now and then, but that Dr Tupper has so set me at ease about your health, that I am quite comfortable on that subject. I am quite well — the heat seems to have acted so far, as a salutary alternative. I am much less oppressed here, than I was in the deep valleys of Switzerland. At Pfaffers, I think, I could not live a day. At Sargans, Ragatz, Coire, &c., &c., a week would knock me up. Trust me, I have especial care of myself. I fear what I wrote on Saturday and have written today, is too small. I will not do so again. It is too bad for your eyes — leave it till my return, and I will read it to you myself. I shall not, probably, have time to commit the same fault again; for we must make the best of our way back to Switzerland after having been at Venice and Milan. Mrs and Miss B(arlow) beg me to give their best remembrances, and desire me not to forget to say, we often talk of you. My best love to my father and Marian when you write. Ever, my dear aunt, very affectionately yours,

A.L. -

Letter from Anne Lister (senior), dated from Paris, 6 July 1827, to her niece, Anne Lister, at Berne.

... I was exceedingly pleased, and gratified, my dear Anne, with your very amusing and satisfactory letter, you may believe it is a great comfort to me, to have it under your own hand that you are *well* — do not think of writing me another *long* letter, it will occupy too much of your time. I am not so selfish as to wish it, after the fatigue of the day, and writing your Journal, you will require all the rest you can get. A few lines to say you are *well*, will quite satisfy me, as I hope and trust you get such comfortable sleep at night as to prevent you suffering in the least from the exercise you may be induced to take in the day. I think of you very *very* often, and drink the health of 'The Travellers' every day after dinner ... I keep my accounts very regular, and send George to the Halle for vegetables, but I do not indulge myself with much fruit, it is so bad, the cherries I have had, looked well, and quite ripe, but on tasting them, found them so old and dry, they might have been off the tree at least a week, I then tried strawberries — they asked forty sols a basket in the shops, George got a beautiful looking basket at the Halle for twenty-eight sols. I fancied he had got them remarkably cheap, and that I should have a great treat of strawberries and cream after dinner, but you may imagine my disappointment, when on removing those on the outside, I found the rest small, crushed, and some quite mouldy. I am more and more convinced, that unless you can see everything with your own eyes, you are continually liable to deception. The weather has occasionally been very oppressive, that I felt to want a little rummage, and fresh air, and determined to take a drive in the Bois de Boulogne for a couple of hours. As it would be more agreeable with a companion, I went on Wednesday evening to ask Mrs Droz to accompany me the day following (Thursday last) ...

Anne Lister, dated from Varese, 16 August 1827, to her aunt in Paris.

... As I have said before, we were all delighted with Venice — we returned by Padua, Mantua, Cremona, and Lodi to Milan, a very interesting route. We were charmed with the Lake of Como, and cannot fancy that any lake anywhere can please us better, if so well. Of course, we went to Villa d'Este the residence of our unhappy queen Caroline. I shall say nothing about the place, having bought a description of it which you will see. We made all the inquiries we could — I mean to say nothing about it to people in general; but, unfortunately, we heard quite enough to persuade us, our King was quite right not to suffer such a queen to be the crowned queen of England. She left Villa d'Este, a very lovely place, and went to Pesaro because the Emperor of Austria would not allow Bergami[5] to wear his orders in the Austrian dominions. I by mistake told both Mariana and Isabella that he allowed his wife only five francs a day — I ought to have written 20/-. He is now living at Pesaro, wallowing in the riches derived from the queen's infatuation. Majocchi is now a horse-dealer at Milan. We left Como with regret — the air so delightful — the lake so beautiful. Fine drive from there to Lugano, and we were agreeably surprised to find the Lake of Lugano much finer than we expected. From Lugano here, is singularly beautiful. It strikes us as being altogether the most beautiful drive we have seen since leaving Paris. I longed for you to have been with us on the Lake of Como. It would have reminded you a little of the best part (of) Winandermere. We are all sorry to leave Italy.

Geneva, 27 August, 1827

Anne Lister to her aunt in Paris.

... Tell Isabella we were much pleased with the village of Clarens, and sat an hour in the house where Lord Byron would be taken and spent two or three days. A young lady who went the other day, kissed his bed twenty times — the house his lordship had at Coligny, near here, seemed to us the loveliest situation hereabouts. Lady Byron went to the house at Clarens; but the old woman was from home, had taken the key of the room with her, and her ladyship could not see it. Lord B —

---

[5] Bartolomeo Bergami was engaged at Milan, in 1814, as a courier by Queen Caroline (1768-1821). She was tried before the Lords in 1820. charged with adultery with Bergami. Majocchi was probably the coachman.

seems to have been much liked by the people around here — the old woman told us, she had cried like a child when she heard of his death ...

Anne Lister to her aunt in Paris.

Berne, Tuesday night 11 September, 1827.

... I may not have an opportunity (of) visiting this country again; and as you are really so well, and going on so well, and Isabel so anxious for me not to return on her account, I have at last decided to postpone my return home. That I inadvertently omitted giving you the key of the wine cellar fidgets me — it is in my carriage-seat box — your key will open it. You can get the key out yourself, and desire George to bring up what wine you want. It is much the least trouble to borrow money for the time on Isabella's credit — she cannot be inconvenienced — Lafitte will advance her what she wants; and you will repay her immediately on my return. We went from Geneva to Chamounix — astonished with Mt Blanc — tired ourselves out on the Mer de Glace — crossed the Tête Noire to Martigny — stopt at the hospice on the Great St Bernard, thanked our stars when we were safe back again, returned by the south side of the lake of Geneva, thence to Neuchâtel, the lake of Bienne, and Rousseau's little Isle of St Pierre, and thence here, surely the prettiest town in Europe. The walks and drives are magnificent — thought of Isabella on the Engi, and all wished you and she were with us. The people are civil — the shopkeepers take no advantage of strangers — persons and things are alike neat and clean — the city — the country — the cottages — the costumes — all are picturesque and charming. We have engaged our guide, and are to be off at six tomorrow for Thun, the lakes, cascades, &c., &c., all that Isabella can wish. I hope the fine weather will last us out, and that, on leaving Switzerland, we shall have left little unseen. You shall hear from me once or twice more, but shall not name any day for your seeing for fear of disappointing you. Isabella must positively make room for me, she must pack as en voyage, so that you need not trouble yourself about contriving a bed — tell her, I hope she is not enlarged since I saw her last. I gave her directions to Baute in Geneva who promised to do his best. His shop is a very good,

111

but a very dear one. We are none of us much taken with Geneva; nor do the natives and the English at present get on very well together. The more I see of the continent, the more I am convinced that, take it all in all, there is no place like Paris for a fixed residence. Italy for climate — Berne for English cleanliness — Vevay for the society of Miss Maclean's very agreeable friend Mrs Falconet Fairholme — Mme Carbonier was delighted to see us at their pretty country house a couple of leagues from Neuchâtel. Captn Droz's sister whom we saw in Paris was in the country — I am glad you asked Mme Droz to go out with you in the carriage — but, as you observe, it seems as if there was some spell against her entering it. We were at Hoffwyl yesterday, and exceedingly interested — M. Fellenberg's[6] second son shewed us all over, and was most attentive. You remember what a noise was made by Mr Brougham's letters on the subject of this school. But I must not sit up longer. Again my best love to Isabella — I would write to her but really have not time. I shall be delighted to find her mother's letter at Lucerne. Mrs and Miss B(arlow) beg their best remembrances. I have told them Isabella is a decided blue stocking. Perhaps a little more mountain-work may thin me a little. At present, I am, for me, quite fat. I hope you will get this letter about the 18th. If you have any letters for me from Mariana will you forward them to Geneva, poste restante there — but do not send any off later than the 20th or 21st of this month. We shall be obliged to return here — stay a day, then hurry to Geneva whence we shall take the Diligence to Lyons — stay one day there, and then make the best of our way home … I can no more. Ever, my dear aunt, very affectionately yours,

A.L. -

After Miss Lister's return to Paris she received a letter from her father, containing Halifax news.

Letter from Captain Jeremy Lister, to his daughter Anne.

---

[6] M. Fellenberg's school at Hoffwyl. *see* Encyclopaedia of Education, ed. Paul Monroe, 1911. Vol 2. PP. 590-591. For the correspondence concerning Brougham's visit to the school *see* The Edinburgh Review, 1818-1819, vols 31 and 32.

Shibden Hall. December 8 1827.

My dear Anne,

Marian desired Dr Kenny to write to you as he would be better able to give you a more satisfactory account of her than I could. In the spare paper I take the opportunity of acknowledging the receipt of your letter of November 30, by which I am glad to find both you and my sister are so well. I expect before you receive this you will have had a letter from Mr Briggs respecting Northgate House &c. and I saw Mr Parker yesterday afternoon who informs me our Vicar &c. have been viewing the upper end of Northgate Cabbage Lane field with the view of Building a Church there. I told him I thought there could not be much objection if a fair and reasonable price was given for it and he would write to you on the subject today. I have got paid for the Land they have taken for Godley Lane on Northowram Road in Willroyd brow 1,900 yards at 6½ per yard £51.9.2. agreeable to Mr S. Washington's Valuation and measurement. I have heard nothing further; since my last Letter respecting the other Road speculations. Report says our Vicar has commenced his demand for tithes of Milk &c. on Mr Stansfield of Field House, Mr Goodall of Skircoat, Mr Austler of Fixby, Mr Binns of Norland and Mr Pitchforth of Rastrick so that we shall have plenty of Law and full employment for our Solicitors. After all England may have as many or perhaps more attractions for a permanent Residence than most other Countries, at least from your account Switzerland is not a very favorable Country in your Ideas, had it been our native place your Ideas would in all probability been very different, even Italy I think must give up the palm to old England. Marian joins me in best love to you and my sister and I am
Dear Anne
Yours very affectionately
Jery Lister.

9

PARIS — AN EMBASSY BALL — BELGIUM AND GERMANY

1829-1830

Anne Lister's friendship with Vere Hobart led to her introduction to the latter's aunt, the Hon. Lady Stuart, of the Lodge, Richmond Park, and her son and daughter-in-law, Lord and Lady Stuart de Rothesay. At this time Lord Stuart de Rothesay was the English Ambassador in Paris, thus Miss Lister found herself moving in diplomatic circles when she got to Paris. This trip to the continent was to be the longest she had hitherto undertaken, and she was to travel in Belgium, Germany, the Netherlands, the Pyrenees, and the south of France.

Two days after her arrival in Paris Miss Lister received the following invitation to attend a soirée on the anniversary of King George IV.

L'AMBASSADEUR D'ANGLETERRE
et Lady STUART DE ROTHESAY prient
Miss Lister
de leur faire l'honneur de venir
passer la soirée chez eux le jeudi 30 Avril.

Annivre de Sa Majesté Britannique.

Les Messieurs seront en uniforme
ou en habit habillé.

This magnificent ball is fully described in Miss Lister's journal, where there is also to be found an extract from a letter to Mrs Mariana Lawton, describing the celebration more briefly:- Magnificent! The supper the most splendid thing I ever saw. 2,000 persons invited, and all that suite of rooms full. In spite of such a numerous assemblage the supper was really *good*, and nobody wanted a change of plates or anything. Never saw such order. We had all sorts of things hot and cold that were proper for supper — pines, peaches, strawberries, &c., &c. all sorts of fruit. The plateau and gold ornaments, and natural flowers, and many silver plate magnificent — no china to be seen — all, all plate. Titles English and foreign, stars, garters, &c., &c., a brilliant assemblage. I went with the Cte and Ctesse de Noé. He wore his orders, and looked a very courtly beau — she all civility to your humble servant. Capital people to be with, knowing everyone. Never was I so *entourée de noblesse*. Poor Cameron has not two ideas of Parisian toilette. I had Mme de Conté (Mlle Aspasie that was) to dress me — black gauze over black satin, and chapeau de bal with bird of paradise plumes. Said by Mrs B(arlow) to have entered the rooms with an air distingué, and to have been *très bien accueillie* par Mme l'Ambassadrice who was a blaze of diamonds. Miss Hobart was dancing with the Duc de Chartres[1]; but it was impossible to get near her; and I literally had never an opportunity of speaking to her, for came away at two, not venturing to stay later, not knowing, if we did, when we could get the carriage up. We went early (at ten), and were near an hour in the line of carriages before we could get into the court(yard).

Among the letters of this period are numerous little notes from friends in Paris — Vere Hobart, Madame de Rosny, Countess Galvani, and others; they consist mainly of invitations and plans to meet. A little note, written in July 1829 by Lady Stuart, in which she asks Miss Lister to look over her books, and asks 'the price of floating down the Rhine', is one of the first in this collection of letters to be enclosed in an envelope. The latter is small (3 ¾ ins. by 2 ⅜ ins.); it was not gummed, but was sealed

---

[1] Duc de Chartes (1810-1842), son of Louis Philippe.

with a wafer.

During this stay in Paris Miss Lister attended a course of lectures in science, from April to July, at the Jardin des Plantes; the course included lectures on chemistry, botany, mineralogy (by M. Nérée Boubée[2] and M. Pelletier), and the comparatively new science of geology. The following note, announcing the date of a series of lectures on shells, was written by Jean Victor Audouin,[3] who became professor of entomology at the Paris Museum in 1833.

BIBLIOTHEQUE
de l'Institut Royal de France

* * *

Paris, le 4 juin 1829.
M. Audouin professeur a l'honneur
de présenter ses hommages respectueux à
Mme Lister et de la prévenir qu'il commençera
son cours sur les Coquilles Mardi 9 juin
a 10h ½ très précises *dans les Galeries du*
Museum d'histoire Naturelle.

The following letters relate to the excursion made by Miss Lister and her Paris friends, through Belgium, and down the Rhine.

Anne Lister (Paris? August 13 1829?) to the Honourable Lady Stuart in Paris.

My dear Madam,

I send you the enclosed list of hotels, posts, and prices, as it is possible Henry may not have one to spare, and you may like to have one yourself.

---

[2] Nérée Boubée (1806-1863), French geologist.
[3] Jean Victor Audouin (1797-1841), French entomologist.

I fancy I shall be before you; and, as I quite agree with Lady Stuart de Rothesay, that it would be better for the one to be a little before the other, on account of rooms, I shall not loiter by the way *en attendant*. I hope we shall manage the 9½ posts to Compiègne in ten hours including stoppages. Do you not think I had better set off at nine or earlier, that you may have a better chance of finding everything comfortable on your arrival? Is there anything in particular you would like me to order. Such good tea as we had on Tuesday, you will probably not taste again till you return home. I hope you are quite well today.

I am, my dear Madam, very truly yours,
A. Lister.

Hotel de Bavillet. Compiègne.
Saturday 15 August, 1829.

I hope, my dear aunt, you had a good night last night, and that you are better this morning. I shall be glad to find a line or two from you at Bruxelles. I should not have written to you from here — it would have been rather too little advanced on our journey, had I had all I wanted — but George unaccountably left behind the great front pocket of the carriage, and you can have no idea of the insufferable difference this makes. The forgetfulness was bad enough; but you will guess my surprise and annoyance on his telling me, I had said I did not want it. This has really disappointed me, but I shall say not much about it, or about anything else for the moment. All I wish at present is to remedy the evil as well as I can, and have the thing sent after me. Will you be good enough to . . . send if off by the diligence. By the way, it must be put in a little box, and will you ask Mrs B(arlow) to see the conducteur, if she can, and explain what it is she is sending, and why. It would be best to write a little note to the custom-house officers, to say, that the bag belongs to the carriage of Mme Lister who is gone on before . . . My love to Jane, and thanks for the tippet which I shall not sport till we get to Bruxelles. We got here at six thirty last night — not very good doings — but we all behave admirably. Lady S(tuart) walked about with us for near an hour after our arrival. She is really very good, and already begins to shew the good effect of having travelled much when young. Most other people would have grumbled loudly at our dinner. She asked very particularly how you were, and hopes I shall have good accounts at B(ruxelles). We are just going to breakfast, and be off to the palace. Tonight we sleep at St Quentin. Cameron *framed* very well. It rained more or less all the way to Senlis but it was fine afterwards, and we had a charming drive down upon Verberie along the beautiful valley of the Autonne, and the forest of Compiègne. Breakfast waits — had I my great bag, I shd be quite comfortable. As it is the carriage is in constant litter, like the carriages of most other people which is insufferable. Good bye, my dear aunt. I shall write as soon as I get the bag at B(ruxelles). At present, I am in great haste. I only hope you are better, and are likely to go on well. Say all that is civil for me to Mr and Mrs W. — and Miss Edwards — how happy I should have been, &c., &c. Ever, my dear aunt, affectionately yours,

A.L. -

Brussels. Sunday 23 August, 1829.

We arrived here, my dear aunt, on Wednesday evening, after having had a very pleasant journey. Not having rooms bespoken for us here, we had the inconvenience of being put where we could not remain, and were therefore so busy settling ourselves &c., &c. on Thursday, that I did not go to the bank till Friday, and consequently did not till then get your letter, and the two letters from Miss McL(ean), and the box containing the great bag, all which arrived quite safe, and were waiting for me. Your account of yourself is quite as good as I expected . . . It does not appear, that there is the least chance of Miss McL(ean)'s meeting us at Rotterdam, therefore no chance of my taking her back with me. She still, however, talks of being with us by the end of next month, via Boulogne. Her account of herself is tolerable. As for our plans here, they are yet rather unsettled. We talk of being off for Antwerp on Tuesday, thence round by Ghent, and back here again for an hour or two on Thursday, then forward that day by Waterloo to Namur — from Namur on Friday to Liège, from Liège on Saturday to Spa where we shall probably stay a couple of days — thence to Aix la Chapelle where we shall perhaps be on the 31st. We may stay a day or two there, and may be at Cologne on the 2nd or 3rd of next month. From Cologne I hope nothing will prevent our going along the Rhine to Mayence where we may perhaps be on the 5th and 6th of next month. From there I shall go over to Francfort, and you had best direct my letters there, Messrs. Frères Bethmann, à Francfort sur la Maine . . . I can, of course, give you no idea as yet when I shall be at home. All I can say is, I shall not loiter after my travelling companions have left me. We get on exceedingly well — we were pleased with the palace and gardens at Compiègne, with the magnificent subterranean canal of St Quentin, and with the fine cathedral of this latter place. We slept at St Quentin the second night (Saturday 15th inst.) and the next day (Sunday) being very rainy, we only went as far as Cambray. Sunday the 17th we slept at Valenciennes where we were interested in seeing the cambric-weaving in the cellars. Tuesday 18th we slept at Mons, a very good town, and Wednesday we got here to dinner. From Valenciennes onwards the country began gradually to put on some faint semblance to England. At Mons we began to have hedges all around the numerous villages, and from Halle to Brussels might be our own dear island with our own coal-pits and steam engines. After having heard so much of Brussels from the Norcliffes, I am in some sort disappointed. Never in my life did I see such a parcel of narrow, winding, crooked streets — there is nothing to form a fine capital but just the quarter where we are — the Place Royale, and the park, and its dependencies. And as for this vaunted park, 'tis but about as large as Grosvenor Square. However, it is certainly very pretty, as far as it goes. The botanic garden is, however, the prettiest I ever saw anywhere; and wonders have been done considering that they only began the thing about a year ago. In short, I can imagine Brussels, like most other English-frequented places on the continent, much improved since the N(orcliffe)s were on the continent. I have not had time to write to any of them, nor shall I till my return . . . Friday and yesterday we went about sight-seeing, and yesterday evening we were at the little theatre in the park, after dining at Lord Orford's. Sir Chs[4] & Lady Bagot are at the Hague, and the Tylors are all at Spa except Mr T. — so that we have not much visiting . . . Today we were at church, went to see the Duke d'Aremberg's fine collection of pictures, and went to the palace Lacken — met the King[5] and one of the princes as we returned. Lord Lindsay spent the evening with us. We have a piano — Miss H(obart) sings charmingly; and I care not if we spend all our time here. Tomorrow is the King's birthday, and we are to have fine fireworks — the *allée verte* is to be illuminated, &c., &c. I would not live here if they would give me the best house in the place, and pay me enough to keep me in magnificence. Yet our Hotel (Bellevue) is very comfortable. We have an excellent apartment au premier, looking on the park. You will guess the house is not small when I tell you, they make up *four hundred beds*. My letter will not go till tomorrow but I hope you will get it on Friday. We have had nothing to complain of but the wet weather, which, as with you, has been cold. Do forward me all the letters you have. You had best send them off immediately to Aix la Chapelle, but if they are not sent off immediately they will be too late to meet me nearer than at Francfort. I cannot add more than that I am always, my dear aunt, very affectionately yours,

A.L. -

Letter from Lady Duff Gordon (Aix la Chapelle), (September 14 1829) to Anne Lister, at L'Hotel du Dragon d'Or, Aix la Chapelle.

Dear Miss Lister,

Are you *still* determined to *start* tomorrow? for I feel very much inclined to join you as you kindly invited me to do. If I do have you room for *me* in your carriage, I paying for a *horse*? and then my son and maid can go per diligence. Le Cour Imperial is the last Inn at Cologne I've been told. And how much money shall I take? And what o'clock shall we go?

Do you think Lady Stuart will not think it unkind my leaving her?

I should have *gone* to you instead of writing this but I'm expecting the Doctor.

---

[4] Sir Charles Bagot (1781-1843), a member of the Privy Council, was sent to the Hague in 1824 to use his influence in securing favourable terms for Belgium, in its separation from Holland.

[5] William I of Holland.

Yours truly,

C.D. Gordon

If the Doctor says it is madness my going I will send you word immediately. I'm sure any *water* will agree better with me than these *Achen-ians*.

Ems. Friday 25 September 1829.

It seems an age, my dear aunt, since my writing to you from Bruxelles. We did all I told you we intended — went to Waterloo, thence by Namur and thro' the beautiful valley of the Meuse to Liège, thence by the almost equally beautiful road to Spa, where we staid a few days, and thence to Aix la Chapelle, where I hoped to have found a letter from you. It was some comfort to get Mariana's letter redirected by yourself, so that I guessed from your handwriting you were well. At all rates, I made up my mind to take no news for good news. In this way I went on very quietly for the few days of my stay at Aix la Chapelle; but Lady S(tuart) being so strongly advised to try the waters there for ten days or a fortnight, that she at last consented, I grew tired of waiting for the letters I expected at Francfort, and left Lady S(tuart) to wait my return, and set off with Lady Gordon and her son, and got my letters on Monday morning. Still no letter from you. How could this be? I should have been glad of one single line from you or Mrs Barlow. But again the redirection of the two letters (one from Mr Waterhouse, one from Mr Briggs) was in your own handwriting; and I again hoped, that all was well in Paris. The letters were to say, that all proceedings about the lower road by Lower brea had been stopt, because my father would have it, that my consent was conditional, depending upon whether the trustees could give me full possession of the old road. Of course, I wrote immediately, explaining that I certainly did not wish to have anything to do with the exec(uto)rs of Mr Walsh, but that as for the ground wanted at Lower brea, if they would take all things fairly into consideration and give me a fair value for the land taken and the damage done, I should be satisfied. I fear my father will not quite like this, but, between ourselves, I would rather have the road in front of the house, than at the back as authorized by the act, and therefore am not intending to make any

121

unnecessary opposition. As for the old road, it will stop itself in time, when there is a better. I had not time to write to my father by the same post, but begged Mr Briggs to communicate to him the substance of what I had written. I should have written to you, but somehow we were all in such a bustle (it was Francfort fair) that I really could not. We left Francfort on Wednesday, slept that night at Mayence, slept yesterday at Swalbach, and arrived here between four and five this afternoon. It is one of the prettiest watering places we ever saw — on the banks of the Lahn, about two hours' drive from Coblentz. We stay here tomorrow to see the environs, mean to sleep at Coblentz on Sunday — at Cologne on Monday, and get back to Aix la Chapelle on Tuesday. What we shall all do next I cannot say till I have seen Lady S(tuart) but will write as soon as anything is fixed. I begin to be anxious to get home again. I get anxious to know how you are, and I should not like Mrs B(arlow)'s being obliged to go before my return .... . Lady G(ordon) and I have really had a pleasant little tour. She is a friend of Lady S(tuart)'s — we met at Aix la Chapelle, and have gone on very well together. We went as far as Darmstadt, and went to the opera there on Sunday last. Admirable orchestra, beautiful scenery and dresses, but bad singing. Francfort is a capital town; and we all regretted not being able to stay longer than two days. The scenery along the Rhine is certainly very fine between Coblentz and Bingen, but one's expectations are always raised to such a height it is always impossible not to be rather disappointed than otherwise. Perhaps, having heard nothing of the road by which we are returning, we are almost as much pleased with it as with the Rhine. Wiesbaden is an uncommonly nice little watering place, and this (Ems) is beautiful. So is Spa; but it seems more out of the way than Ems. I like Aix la Chapelle much better than I expected — we had a nice society there as well as at Spa. But the detail of my travel must be left for conversation on my return. I cannot collect my ideas just now so as to give you any regular account of all we have seen and done ... I dare not tell you where to direct; for I trust we shall all be off from Aix la Chapelle as soon as possible after my return. I shall advise giving up all thought of Holland, in which case I shall probably go with my friends as far as Bruges, and then make the best of (my) way home. You may count on my having much to tell you ... I have never ceased to think of getting something for the B(arlow)s but everything everywhere is French — to be got better, and cheaper, in Paris, and I have been in despair and got nothing as yet. Nothing but French things, in the present-making way, even at Francfort, except a few Vienna workboxes, &c. which I myself do not much admire, and which would only have been lumber to people on the eve of a long journey. The same is to be said of all the things we saw at Spa — French manufacturers are everywhere. I only wish the language was as common. It is absurd to say that French is spoken everywhere on the Rhine. Merely a few Innkeepers speak it, and one has all the difficulty in this world to get on with German. But no more. It is quite bedtime. I only hope you are going on well. Love to Mrs & Miss B. -. Ever, my dear aunt, very affectionately yours,

A.L. -

Letter from Anne Lister, Paris, (drafted by M.T. Leclerq), to le Conte de St Ciran, requesting him to play his bugle in some other part of his hotel as it increases her aunt's sufferings.

Mademoiselle Lister commence par demander pardon à Monsieur le Conte de St Ciran pour la demande qu'ell va lui faire. Elle a une tante fort souffrante dans ce moment ci et que le moindre bruit incommode horriblement. Monsieur de St Ciran doit penser que le cor qui se fair entrendre quelquefois lui augmente les souffrances de cette dame.

S'il lui ètait possible de choisir une autre partie de son hotel pour cet exercice, Mademoiselle Lister en serait extrêmement reconnaissante. Elle supplie Monsieur de St Ciran de croire qu'elle ne s'etre portée à cette démarche que par une indispensable nécessité.

Elle a l'honneur de lui faire ses remercimens d'advance.

Wednesday 21 April 1830.

One afternoon Miss Lister's coachman failed to appear with her carriage to take her to a lecture and she was obliged to walk. On leaving the lecture she met her manservant, George, who informed her that Jacques was drunk. 'Jacques reeling a little on his box,' wrote Miss Lister in her journal. 'At last, opposite No 23 Quai St Michel (I) pulled the check string, meaning to tell Jacques to drive to Perrelet's, but he "turned round with such a drunken face, I asked what was the matter, and this led to my telling him he reeled on his seat. He asked if I thought *il avait bu.* I said *yes, certainly,* and desired him to let George drive. No! he would not ... I said he should not drive me. He then jumped down and seemed as if going to drive off. I said the carriage was mine and he should not drive it. He then threw off his coat and left it with his great coat on the box, took off the horses and led them off. I said little or nothing, but stood quietly by while George got a fiacre. Very civil people at No 23. There was quite a scene ... it seemed the horses I had belonged not to me who paid for them, but to the coachman who drove them ... 'Oh! Oh! said I, I will arrange this better another time; 'tis lucky the thing has happened.' Said I, 'the *loueur de chevaux* ought to pay for the fiacre horses.' As a result of this incident Miss Lister sent a letter (drafted by M. Théodore Leclerq), to a friend, asking him to get her possessions back from Jacques, whom she had dismissed as incompetent. Jacques wrote an apologetic letter a few days later, but Miss Lister was adamant.

Miss Lister's interest in geology had led her to make inquiries of Professor Boubée, and, in a long letter written in French (May 9 1830) the latter offered to lend her his collection of geological specimens, and he quoted his terms for private lessons. To this Miss Lister replied as follows:-

Monsieur, J'ai bien réfléchi à votre lettre et je regrette beaucoup qu'il y ait de si grandes difficultés à suivre l'étude que, je me proposais d'entreprendre sous vos auspices. Je n'ai point acheté la collection dont je vous ai parlé, ni aucun échantillon de quelque part que ce soit. J'ai abandonné pour le moment l'idée de faire une collection moi-meme, et, toute reflexion faite, je ne veux pas du tout vous faire courir les risques du transport de vos beaux échantillons. Il m'est donc impossible maintenant d'aprés ce que je vois de profiter de vos instructions dans un cours particulier. Et quant à votre tres interessant cours publique, j'ai le regret d'avoir formé des arrangemens avant hier qui ne me permettrent pas de le suivre. Je vous remercie beaucoup de m'avoir annoncé le jour ou vous devez commencer vos promenades géologiques. [6] *Recevez, Monsieur, l'assurance de ma parfaite consideration.*

---

[6] *Quelque plaisir que j'eusses a y assister je n'ai pas la certitude de pouvoir le faire ce Lundi 10 Mai 1830.*

10

SIGHT-SEEING IN THE PYRENEES

1830

Tarbes. Monday 2 August 1830.

It is odd enough, my dear aunt, that the letter I wrote you from
Orleans is now lying on my desk. Lady S(tuart) sent it with
hers — the servant at the Embassy immediately sent it back,
instead of sending it to you, and here it is. However, it matters
not much. You will be sure we are all going on well, or you
would have heard of it. I meant to have written from Bordeaux
to you and to Mariana, but the heat was so excessive, it was
more than enough to see the sights we must see, and I did
nothing else. Journal, all in arrear. The thermometer was one
day 96° in the shade, and at 74° the air seemed quite cool. To
begin, however, my history since leaving you, I had an excellent
journey the first day, and reached Orleans at a quarter before
four about half an hour before the rest of the party. The election
not being quite over, we were with difficulty accommodated,
but, tho' really uncomfortably packed for the night, nobody
made the least complaint, and we were off at eight thirty next
morning, and reached Blois our next sleeping place at a quarter
before four. The rest were rather tired, having had too little
sleep the night before leaving home, but I drove off immediately,
a beautiful little excursion into the country, to see the fine old
Chateau of Chambord. Blois a very prettily situated town.
Thence (Thursday 22nd ult.) to Tours a fine drive. No wonder
there are so many English at T -; for it is really a good town
in the midst of a fine rich country where everything is good,

and ought to be moderately cheap. Friday 23 from Blois to Poitiers, a town one needs not say peculiarly interesting to an English person — a few Roman remains, and a druid cromlech and a fine old cathedral which we preferred to those of Orleans, Blois, and Tours. Saturday 24. From Poitiers to a comfortable Inn in the rather picturesque little town of Ruffec. Sunday 25. From Ruffec off between five and six, for here it began to be hot, to Barbezieux. The grasshoppers began to remind us of Italy, and every symptom convinced us of our approach to a hot climate. The weather was, and had been all along, delightful. We sauntered about for a couple of hours till nine and never enjoyed ourselves more than amid the interesting ruins of the old castle. F in the shade 72° at five thirty a.m. got up to 92° at four in the afternoon, and stood at 81° at nine forty-five in the evening. Monday 26. Off from Barbezieux before six, and reached Bordeaux before six in the evening. As hot as the day before — the sight of a capital Inn, and large lofty rooms opening onto a large terrace with a view of the river and shipping, made us congratulate ourselves on our arrival, and fancy we should find three days a time quite short enough for the enjoyment of such luxury. Our consul, Mr Scott, and his family, were all attention. We spent one (evening) at their beautiful country house, and they came to us another, and the evening of our arrival we had but to dine and go to bed. We did what we could the morning and the evening of each day, but mid-day heat seemed the very solvent of life itself, and we had seen all we cared for down to the mummies under the tower of the church of St Michael, and were glad enough to be off before five in the morning on Friday the 30th. No posting in France like that from Paris to Bordeaux. We were perpetually driven at the rate of a post in half an hour. We vainly hoped such might last a little longer, and meant to stay at Agen, but were obliged to stop short at Tonneins, and tho' off at five thirty on Saturday the 31st did not reach Auch till after seven in the evening, — yesterday (Sunday 1 August) meaning only to come here.

Pau. Monday 2 August six thirty p.m. I wrote from Tarbes while waiting for horses — the rest of the party had been off very early — I obliged to wait for my banker. Lady S(tuart) has this moment told me the Paris news. Do pray write immediately and say how you are. Send your letter with your compliments under cover to His Excellency Lord Stuart de

Rothesay, who will forward it. We are perfectly quiet and well off here. You are in no sort of danger but I fear your making yourself uncomfortable. We are all entreated to remain quietly where we are. Do pray write to M — and tell her you have heard from me, but write not one word of politics, or she will never get your letter. I must hasten to say ever, my dear aunt, most affectionately yours,

A.L. -

Lady S(tuart) is sealing her packet and I have not a moment to read over what I have written.

Pau. Wednesday August 4 1830.

This, my dear aunt, is the third time of my writing to you, tho' I fear you cannot as yet have even one of my letters . . . You would conclude that we should be informed as late as possible of what was going on in Paris;[1] and it was not till our arrival here on Monday that we were aware of the real state of things. Surely, surely, you would be as calm, and as little alarmed as possible under such circumstances. The horrors were not in our street; and I have, at least, the comfort of knowing that you would be *comparatively* undisturbed, for you were, at least, spared the sight of carnage. I am sure our worthy proprietor would do all he could to calm and reassure you, and I anxiously hope to hear that you have gone on even better than might have been expected. All is quiet now; and we have the satisfaction of hearing our compatriots highly praised for their great humanity and kindness to the wounded. They say, the post, the letters will be henceforth uninterrupted. I hope, therefore, you will get this, and that letters to England will also go safe. But do write a few lines to Mary (of course you have written to Shibden) to say that we are all well, and to set her at ease. She as well as all our friends in England will probably have been under great alarm. I entreat you to write to me immediately on your receipt of this. You will have written thro' Lord Stuart, but write again, if but a line or two, by the post directed to me Poste restante, à Pau, Basses-Pyrenées. I shall not feel at all at ease till I have heard from you. I have not once as yet thought of hastening my return — in the first instance, return was next to impossible; and, in the next, we were already advised not to think of it.

I shall decide nothing till I hear what you wish; but, at least for the present, I am strongly persuaded of the propriety of staying quietly where we are. Our moving-about plans are, of course completely set aside just now. We are lucky to be in an exceedingly comfortable house, in a very quiet town, and in every respect very well off. There are several English families here, and the great wish of the inhabitants seems to be to prevent their going away. Almost all the good houses in the country neighbourhood are occupied by our compatriots, said to be seventy families, besides many individuals. I am glad we have done nothing on this tremendous occasion to make ourselves otherwise than liked in Paris, and I do hope that nothing will occur to interrupt this good understanding between the two countries. We hear that the publication of *Galignani's Messenger* was only interrupted for a couple of days. This will inform you of all events of importance; and I trust that you need be under no further alarm. I wish you would desire Macdonald to speak to M. Leclercq if at home, if not, to the porter, to try and get me the *Journal des Débats* French newspapers from the beginning of last month, and to subscribe to it for three months, as I shall be anxious to see this journal on my return home. Do not write politics, but let me know how you were, and how you felt, and how you went on during the terrible days when all must have been in confusion, shops shut, and people hardly able to provide each other with the necessaries of life. All this time we were travelling quietly along without inconvenience of any kind as you will see from my note of Monday, in which was a history of ourselves up to that day, and our arrival here. It is a beautiful place, and we are very comfortably settled till such time as it is judged expedient for us to move. When this will be we have none of us much idea, but direct here till you hear to the contrary; for, should we move sooner than seems likely at present, our letter will be forwarded. I almost hope you have heard from Mariana. How is Mme de Hagemann? Do gave my best regards to her when you see her. Ever, my dear aunt, very affectionately yours,

A.L. -

---

[1] The publication on 25 July 1830, by Charles X, of three ordinances, incited the people of Paris to armed insurrection in order to assert their sovereignty. The Revolution lasted from July 27-29 and resulted in the downfall of the Bourbons.

Paris. Monday 9 August 1830.

I have received your letter, my dear Anne, but it is too late I fear to return an answer by this day's post, as it is near three o'clock, however it will go tomorrow, and I am the less anxious about it as you would get my little note from the Embassy, and that I hope would set you quite at ease on my account. It is odd enough that your first letter should not reach my hands, and that it was by mere chance that I opened the second, it was brought late in the evening, and seeing it directed to you, I was going to put it quietly away, till I knew where to send it, but being a little torn near the seal, I accidentally discovered your handwriting, and you may be sure lost no time in opening, and reading its contents, which did me a wonderful deal of good. As it distresses my eyes to write by candle light, I did not attempt it and I had scarcely begun the next morning, when my letter was sent for. Before I proceed further, let me entreat you, my dear Anne, not to think of returning, there is no need whatever for you to do so, when I tell you, I am tolerably well; and now quite composed, that it would be foolish indeed in me to wish your return a day sooner than you think advisable or necessary. Of course your plans cannot be arranged just yet, when they are, let me know. I am glad you have got so comfortable a house, and hope you are less inconvenienced by the heat of the weather than you were. It is much cooler here since a tremendous storm of thunder and lightning, hail and rain, which awoke me betwixt two and three o'clock on Thursday morning, and continued without intermission for near an hour, my room as light as day from the incessant flashes of lightning and the loud peals of thunder were truly awful. The horrors of the several preceding days, might perhaps cause me to be rather more nervous than I usually am during a thunder storm. I, at first, thought they were firing cannon in the street, which had been threatened, when barricading it. I however soon recollected that there was no occasion for alarm, as all had been quiet and the people walking about the evening before ... I hope and trust the French people will now be as happy as they have been the contrary. The Duke of Orleans is to be proclaimed King today — he will be Philip the first[2]. You ask me to tell you how I felt, and how I went on during the terrible days, but now that is all over; it is best to say nothing about it ... I fear I will trespass sadly on your time to read so long a letter, but I will only add, my best love, and sincere good wishes for your health, which I hope is better than when you went, say in your next, if change of air has done you good. I am, my dear Anne, very affectionately yours,

Anne Lister. (Senior)

Pau. Saturday 14 August 1830.

I am just returned from a little excursion among the mountains, and am delighted, my dear aunt, to have received your note. It was a wonder mine had any direction at all; for, in my hurry, I gave it, as I recollected afterwards, to Lady Stuart de Rothesay undirected, and thus it arrived in Paris. I have not more time to answer yours than you had to answer mine. I will write again as soon as we are settled at St Sauveur (Hautes Pyrénées) where we expect to sleep on Monday. We leave here tomorrow ...

A.L. -

St Gervais. August 28 1830.

My dear Miss Lister,

I do feel very desirous to hear how your aunt is after all that has passed in Paris, were you returned from the Pyrenees? Notwithstanding your professions I must so far touch upon politics as to say I sincerely hope all things will remain quiet, and that noble acting may be continued, and wise yielding to good government may follow up valiant fight for freedom from despotism. I hope we may go into Italy this winter, what think you, now do answer me according to the best of your judgement, which you well know, or ought to know, I do not consider the worst in the world, do not be so horribly diplomatic as you were in a letter written some time since in answer to a remark I made upon the detestable Polignac ministry, and the despotism of

---

[2] Accession of Louis Philippe, August 7 1830.

the ex-King. I wish the party may not plant themselves in England, very glad William 4th reigns instead of George 4th!!! ? ... F. P(ickford).

Letter from Mrs Ann Norcliffe, to Anne Lister at Toulouse.

6 September 1830.

My dear Miss Lister,

I should have written sooner to you had I known where to direct, but as I imagined the late events in Paris, as soon as they reached your ears would cause your return there, I delayed it, and was not a little anxious till a letter from your good aunt convinced me she had not suffered in health from what must have been to a nervous person particularly unpleasant. Thank God all is now quiet and peaceable and I trust may continue so. We have nothing to do with it except as far as wishing peace, and quiet to every country, I hope it may be a means of keeping many of our own countrymen at home, to spend their money where it is much wanted, amongst their own people. I lament much for the injury committed to dear Bruxelles,[3] a place I must ever love and the people's kindness to our wounded can never be forgot. Thank God we are all quiet in England, and we should be ungrateful if we are not satisfied and happy. We have been very busy with our elections. The city one went as we wished, and the unsuccessful candidate conducted himself in the most gentlemanly good-humoured (manner), and all animosity ceased with the chairing; it was a difficult situation for him as he was High Sheriff, Lord Mayor, and unsuccessful candidate. Our County election lowered us much as a County, but it is now over and York is returned to its usual quiet, and had it not been for the arrival of Madame Vestris[4] (which event tempted *even* Mrs Duffin, and her husband to the theatre) would have continued so. The only topic of conversation was about some beautiful pillars found under the present choir of the Minster, and which belonged to the first Cathedral, only two are there, the other two have been taken to make the present crypt. The pillars are like those in the cathedral at Durham, and the choir has been much longer and narrower than the present one. We succeeded I hope in preventing the present one being removed.

The other topic of conversation was the intended marriage of the Dean to a Miss Pearse ... With my kind regards to your aunt believe me most truly yours,

Ann Norcliffe.

Bagnères-en-Bigorre. Monday night 13 September 1830. I said I would write to you, my dear aunt, as soon as we[5] were settled at St Sauveur. I fully meant to do so, but somehow I was so perpetually making one little excursion or another, and so busy, or so tired and sleepy, that the time slipped away before I was aware of it, and we were off to Cauteretz, and from there here before I had written one line of all I intended ... the fact is, your little note thro' the Embassy, set at rest my great anxiety, and I did not fidget myself any more, or have another thought about returning before the time. Thank you and M. Leclercq about the newspaper. I only regret the impossibility of getting the numbers published during the memorable month of July ... How could you fancy it would 'trespass sadly on my time to read so long a letter'? The longer the better. Having time to read and time to write, are two totally different things. I have heard two or three times from Lady S(tuart) and have just been writing to her. I shall copy what I have told her about our journeyings. You may like to see it, and I can make it more complete by and by, by word of mouth. On the subject of Pau: It is certainly a charmingly situated town, but we grew tired of it, and were delighted to get among the high mountains. We went over to see Eauxbonnes, and Eaux Chaudes, about a couple of hours drive the one from the other, and each about six hours from Pau. At E.B. there was still a little remnant of society that political events had spared for a few days longer than the rest — M. and Mme de Boisjelin, M. and Mme Charles de Goutant, & M. & Mme Eynard — but the poor people of the place were all lamenting, in concert with all the people of all the other

---

[3] Revolution of Belgium, August 1830. Disturbances began on 25 August 1830, the people demanding the administrative separation of Holland and Belgium. The result was the dissolution of the Kingdom of the Netherlands in December 1830.

[4] Madame Lucia Elizabeth Vestris (1797-1856), English actress.

[5] Anne was travelling with Lady Stuart de Rothesay and her children.

watering places, over their season spoilt, and all that they had lost. The ten or a dozen houses of E.B are built so entirely at the end of the little valley, and at the foot of huge mountains seeming to forbid escape, that we felt as if immured in prison, and waited patiently for horses a day longer than we intended. We thought E.C. the prettier of the two, perhaps because it was not in such a cul-de-sac, but in a deep, narrow valley forming one of the many magnificent passes into Spain. We spent another day or two, *en passant*, at Pau, were perhaps ungrateful on bidding it adieu with so little regret, and arrived in one day's beautiful drive at St Sauveur, I on Sunday, and the rest on Monday 15 and 16 of last month, dividing our party for fear of being delayed in these little places for want of horses. Our comfort at St Sauveur spoilt us for everywhere else. Never were headquarters more generally approved; and we spent three weeks there, and did the main business of bathing and drinking the waters without a moment's impatience for other and newer scenes. We rode, walked, and were carried about most luxuriously in *chaises à porteur*. Only two carriage-roads, that by which we came, and that to Barèges and back — the wonder is there should be any at all — the latter being more or less destroyed every year by the furious torrent of the Bastan, and the former being very nearly the whole way from Pierrefitte to Luz (a distance of two posts) a *vraie* Corniche, twelve or fourteen feet wide, cut along first one side then the other of the magnificent mountain gorge — we congratulated ourselves on not being ordered to Barèges. One plot of wood, raised(?) up to shade some zig-zag walks, is all the shelter there is. The rest is black, savage mountain; and so dreadful are the avalanches, the town is deserted in winter save by four or five people who are provisioned, and confined there till the return of summer, instances being named of some of them having been devoured, in the mean time, by bears or wolves. Even our pretty little town of St Sauveur (about twenty houses) is nearly deserted in the winter, the inhabitants retiring to Luz, the lively little capital of its own and the adjoining vallies. Our excursion to Gavarnie took one long day. It was *something* to see the highest cascade in Europe (1,266 feet), the magnificent Cirque of marble rock, the *brêche de Roland*, and so much that legends of romance have famed. I could not resist mounting a little higher than the rest, and retraced the Duchesse de Berri's to the *brêche*, and went beyond them to the summit of Mt Perdu. When one hears that Raymond (Roland?) failed twice before he could succeed., it seems as if I had done a great thing — but he had the way to find, and would attempt it from the north side, and had more difficulties to encounter than those who were to follow him by the southern, and the easier side. I do not, however, mean to say, the ascent was without difficulty, tho' it was certainly more fatiguing than difficult. The view was magnificent, particularly towards Spain. It was not, however, entirely for the view I had gone up — I was curious to try the effect of the air at so great an elevation, but none of the inconveniences so often complained of, affected me at all. I felt only that the breeze was light and exhilarating. I forgot that I had passed a sleepless night in the miserable *cabane* of a Spanish shepherd, that we had had four hours of laborious ascent, and that from the setting off by candle-light at a quarter past three in the morning, I had had no breakfast. It was the perfect solitude, the profound stillness that gave me a sensation I had never had before — there was no trace of living thing — no sound that reached the ear, for even the very waters were too far below us to be heard. The sunshine raised Fahrenheit to 38° even lying on the glacier that covers the northern declivity of the summit. It was half an hour before I became sensible that the wind was cold and it was time to descend. We were down in three hours, and then made the best of our way along the magnificent gorge d'Ortessa and val de Broto to the picturesque little town of Torla. We might have been in the very heart of Spain, so different was all we saw on that side of the mountain from all that we had left on the other — the Spanish shepherds, always knitting, and the peasantry in general are handsome, and much more picturesque than the French. The low, round-crowned, enormous-brimmed Arrangonese hat is certainly more picturesque than the high Barèges cap, or Bèarn bèret; and the fine black eyes, and long black braided hair of the women made me even forget the scarlet capulet bound with black, that gives so highly picturesque an appearance to every paysanne here. I was most hospitably received by the receiver of customs, and, declining meat, supped on good bread, and wine like cordial, and large delicious grapes — they gave me excellent chocolate for breakfast. The receiver himself shewed me about the little town. The priest came to pay his respects; and we contrived to understand each other in Latin.

134

He immediately asked if I was *christiana*. I guessed there was but one step in Spain from christian or Roman Catholic to heretic or infidel, and said yes. This opened to me every drawer of the sacristy, and even the very pipes of the organ, a man being sent for to let me hear the fine tone. The church, tho' small was a very good one — the neatly fresco-painted interior glittering in all directions with gilded cornices and saints. I must not, however, forget to tell you, that, to the no small fright of the guide, the first person who had awaited my getting up in the morning was a Captain of engineers, in full uniform, who had come from Broto (four or five miles off) and must see me immediately, the police having been informed that I had been *drawing military plans!* You would have laughed to see the careful examination of my little note book. But the Signor di Garcia was really a gentleman, saw at once that I was neither Mina[6] in disguise, nor probably any other than my passport declared me to be, wrote me a curious little certificate of assurance that he found my papers unexceptionable, said I should find the country perfectly tranquil, and it was a great pity I should not go, at least, to Saragossa. I almost regretted that I could not, but promised myself a little tour in Spain the first good opportunity. It was about noon when the mules came to the door, and we were off for Bouchero and the Port de Gavarnie. We had halters twisted into bridles, and great wooden shoes with the heels cut off for stirrups, and such grotesque looking saddles, my gravity could stand it no longer. The piles of fine fir timber we saw to be dragged down to Torla, and thence floated to Madrid, seemed merely to have thinned the forests a little in places. Bouchero is merely a single house or hospice, and here, for the first time in my life, I saw a large raised hearth in the middle of the room, three great burning fir trees lying across it, by which the people were cooking dinner, and the smoke escaping from a large hole in the middle of the roof. Six peasants were just sitting down to a yellowish-brown looking hash swimming in gravy, that smelt so good, I could not help tasting it. I thought it excellent, tho' they declared it was nothing but oil, and pepper, and salt and, of course, a little saffron. It was dusk when we got back to Gavarnie, and dinner time the following day on our reaching St Sauveur. On Monday we went to Cauteretz, staid till Wednesday morning, and arrived here in the afternoon. On Tuesday we had a delightful excursion to the Pont d'Espagne and lac de Gaube, the only scenery that at all reminded me of what I saw on the Spanish side. We all agreed that as a place to stay at, we should not like Cauteretz near so well as St Sauveur which, I am quite persuaded, is the nicest little town in the Pyrenees, tho' perhaps (next to the waters here) the waters are among the least strong. We are really very comfortable here, but it is quite town life — two-and-twenty streets instead of two-and-twenty houses (if so many) of St Sauveur. Unluckily it rained the day we came, and has rained ever since, that we have not been able to get out much. On Wednesday we shall be off to Bagnères de Luchon — the length of our stay there not fixed, but I suppose about ten days. People seem as if they expected insurrections everywhere, but for that, I believe I would have been tempted to make another little excursion into Spain, into Catalonia; but things, they say, are likely to be worse there than anywhere. We shall probably be at Toulouse on the 26th and at Montpellier on the 30th. When I know beyond this, I will tell you. But good night! I really must go to bed. Ever, my dear aunt, very affectionately yours,

A.L. -

Letter from Anne Lister, dated from Nîmes, 10 October 1830, to her aunt in Paris.

. . . We did not leave Bagnères de Bigorre quite so soon as was intended at the time I wrote to you last. One of the children was ill, and that detained us. She was better, however, in a little while, and we then pursued our plans. I was off before the rest, and made a nice little excursion into Spain where I had the amusement of being escorted by soldiers one day, and stopt by a douanier another. But nothing could answer better than this my second journey into Spain, and in spite of Mina and his guerillas I am quite safe, and never enjoyed anything more. I saw the sources of the Garonne, and was at a Spanish evening party which really entertained me exceedingly. The scenery on

---

[6] Francisco Espoz Y Mina (1781-1836), Spanish General, who began guerilla warfare against the French invaders in 1818. In 1830 he took part in a rising against Ferdinand VII of Spain.

the Spanish side the Pyrenees seems so much bolder and finer than on the French. I fear I have only done enough to sharpen more than ever my wish to see a little more of the peninsular — but all this is, of course, a thing to be talked of by and by rather than thought of now. From Spain I returned to Bagnères de Luchon, thence to Toulouse where we spent two or three days — thence to Montpellier for a couple of days, and arrived here to dinner today. We thought Toulouse rather stupid — Montpellier charming, and are delighted with the antiquities here which are certainly very fine.

Monday evening 11 October. Tomorrow we are to be off very early in the morning to the Pont du Gard, go as far as we can on our road to Marseilles, and sleep there on Wednesday. The length of our stay at Marseilles will depend upon how we like the place — but, at any rate, there will be amusement enough for us for a few days — beyond there our plans are not quite fixed. However, as soon as returning is definitely talked of, I will write tho' but a few lines. I am glad Isabella wrote to inquire after you, which was really the greater attention, as Mrs N(orcliffe) tells me she is more idle than ever about writing. I wonder what they all think about their money in the French funds. I shall be glad of your buying Galignani's account of the three memorable days. You seem to have had a great deal of rain. Here there has been no rain I know not how long. We had a great deal at Bagnères de Bigorre, but the moment we got on the other side the mountains, the weather was beautiful, and there was nothing to complain of but the scorching sun . . . The accounts of poor Miss Maclean are far from good. This business about Mr Long has annoyed her a great deal; and I fear she is little in a state to bear any worry of any kind. Lady Stuart seems to think her much altered, and that she is not likely to do more than get the winter over, if so much . . .

Lyons. Sunday 7 November 1830.

My dear Aunt — I almost forget at the moment from where I wrote to you last — but it is no matter, as I am not going to give you much account of myself now that I hope to see you so soon, but merely to say that we talk of being off from here tomorrow, and of being in Paris this day-week, the 14th. We arrived here in good time on Friday from St Vallier. We left

Tracing of part of the letter dated 10 October 1830
in Anne Lister's handwriting

Hyères on Friday-week, and passed thro' Toulon, and Marseilles. I set off a little earlier than the rest for Vienne, where Mariana was born, and where, for the sake of telling her the more about it, I went all over. But, as you will hear all this in a day or two, I shall not keep coffee waiting to write. I had a letter on Friday from Miss Hobart — very bad account of Miss Maclean. She cannot move from one chair to another without assistance, cannot speak above a whisper, or many words at a time, and coughs a great deal. She however, sleeps pretty well, and may still linger some time, *perhaps* even over the winter. Her sister Breadalbane and uncle Sir Hector are with her . . . I shall surely be with you by six this day week, at all rates, I shall not be later if I can help it, unless delayed for horses, or something or other I hope to be able to avoid . . .

A.L. -

11

DISTURBED EUROPE

1830

The letters of this period which passed between Anne Lister and her friends (many of whom were closely connected with the British Embassy in Paris) reflect the disturbed state of Europe after the revolution of July 1830.

Lady Gordon to Anne Lister.

34 Hertford St,
Thursday 18 November. (1830).

I began a letter to you ten days ago, my dear Miss Lister, but never finished it and so have committed it to the all devouring flames. I am glad now that I did so for events have been thickening upon us since, and my letter now to your (ignorant of English events) ears may be more interesting on your return to Paris. *Ministers are out.* The next question is who is in? *Je ne vous dirai pas.* Lord Grey is sent for, but never were there greater difficulties than he has to encounter — if Lord Palmerston and the Messrs. Grant, in short, the remains of the Canning party, will not join him, as they and they only are men of business, real *red tape* men besides their powers of speech in the House of Commons. It is said that everybody, Household and all, excepting the Duke of Buckingham, have resigned, but this I don't believe in the least. The Duke of Wellington has lost himself and his party, by choosing to be presumptuous and to fancy he could do without more strength — everyone of his

Government have long felt the absolute necessity of strengthening themselves. Excepting Sir Robert Peel they were a *laughable* set of *incompetents*. I rejoice at their downfall. If it were not that my brother-in-law, Mr Frankland Lewis, and of course Lord Stuart *falls* with them, it would be without alloy. But those two cases grieve me sorely, and they are both too good and too useful in their very different ways to fall, with such a sett! The Duke has many redeeming merits but as he truly said of himself, 'it was *madness* his attempting to be prime minster of this country'. But a cleaner handed more unjobbing minister never existed, and certainly he has done his possible to lower the expenses of the country . . . We must go to Spain together. I see in you I should find a real *honest* enthusiast, and when once you've been there you will feel as I do — a Spanish corner in your heart, that no other country every takes possession of. I could not resist reading parts of your letters loud to Alexander, and he was so charmed that he is dying to know you and go with you, and thinks perhaps for the *love* of Cosmo, you would let him be your *preux chevalier*. He wants to go there either in the Spring or Autumn. *Nous verrons!* God knows what will become of any of us — one of the FitzClarences[1] has laid a wager that England has no king in five years! An odd wager for the King's son to make methinks! These burnings of ricks and farms continue, and have begun in the north slightly and I had a letter yesterday from Lady Antrobus from Wiltshire saying that they had begun there. The principal of these fires is exactly the same as they were in Normandy — fires that water will not extinguish and certainly not caused by the peasantry themselves. I am very glad that your tour answered so well and that you liked your companions so much. Lady Stuart is a charming and most agreeable companion, and a *very excellent* person besides. Adieu my dear Miss Lister,

Yours most sincerely,

C.D. Gordon

---

[1] The FitzClarences were the illegitimate children of the Duke of Clarence (William IV) and Mrs Dorothea Jordan, the actress.

Letter from Lady Stuart in London, dated November 20, to Anne Lister in Paris.

. . . You will be aware by this time of the terrible state of this country! Indeed it seems fast verging to that of France and the daily accounts of the fires all over the country is decidedly alarming; Mr Baring[2] nearly lost his life and his house is filled (?) with the mob in Hampshire . . . The entire bouleversement of the administration, the Duke of Wellington resigning, &c. has caused more confusion than you can imagine and I hear the King parted with him with the greatest regret and to the last would have done anything to have arranged matters,but he thought it necessary to resign . . . I certainly am all anxiety about Lord Stuart . . .

Letter from Lady Stuart de Rothesay, (Paris November 26 1830).
My dear Miss Lister,

We have nothing but the reports of the town about ourselves, varying according to the suppositions and wishes of our correspondents and their informants. Lord and Lady Granville both declared they knew nothing about Paris for themselves, others say *they* had *declined* and named Sir Fredk Lamb. The fact is that Lord Palmerston does not enter on the duties of office till after his election, so of course nothing can be *true* as nothing can be *fixed*. Will you come and dine with us tomorrow, (Friday) at half past six, you will meet Mrs Hamilton, and some men, but not a case for you to have any of those *cares of toilette* we used to speak of. Ever yours truly,

E. Stuart de Rothesay.

Letter from Lady Stuart de Rothesay, (Paris December 10 1830), referring to the recall of her husband (the British Ambassador in Paris), after the change of ministry in England.

---

[2] Sir Francis Thornhill Baring (1796-1866), liberal member for Portsmouth (1826-1865), Lord of the Treasury (1830-1834), was raised to the Peerage as Baron Northbrook in 1866.

Dear Miss Lister,

We shall *all* stay the winter here, and must take a house instantly. Certainly Lord Granville does not set out *quite* as soon as you say, though he has shewn strange impatience to be here, for in answer to Lord Stuart's request to remain in the Embassy until after the trial, Lord Granville appoints the day on which sentence is to be passed (the 22nd) as the one on which we must give him up the house. It makes it a serious inconvenience to be a *tenant* as well as a servant of Government as no other landlord could give such short notice to quit ... Ever truly yours,

E.S. de R.

Paris. Rue Godot de Mauroy No 39. Monday 20 December 1830.

My dear Mr and Mrs Duffin — to write to you on my return from a journey, has grown into so inveterate a habit, I never feel myself settled at home till I have given you some account of myself while away. You will have read in the papers the death of my poor dear friend Miss Maclean, and this will account to you for my having been at home above a month without having had resolution to sit down and write any letters that were not absolutely necessary. You who knew her, would be aware that I should feel her loss deeply, and would not wonder that it should engross my mind so much. I returned on the 14th ult. and she died on the 16th. The Cromptons will have heard from Breadalbane, and you will have heard from them, that I need not dwell upon the subject, but shall try for your amusement, to turn my thoughts of what I have seen and done since leaving here on the 20th July. That memorable day-week, after having had a pleasant journey by Orleans, Tours, Poitiers, we were at Bordeaux, a very fine town, whose new bridge over the Garonne is unquestionably one of the finest in Europe. It is singular in being hollow, a circumstance arising from the necessity of throwing as little weight as possible upon the piers, and, in consequence of which, you can walk along the inside of the bridge the whole length of it. But one of the most interesting things to see at Bordeaux, is the Asylum, under the care of fourteen *soeurs de charité*. A physican attends when necessary, but that is very seldom. One of the sisters manages the medical department, and I never saw a more neatly arranged physic-room, and better kept laboratory. There were 150 poor patients, half men half women, who paid nothing, and about fifty pay-patients at £48 a year each, each having a little bedroom and sitting-room to themselves. Each division of patients, men, women, gentlemen, and ladies, has its own spacious court and buildings, and there is a large garden which some are allowed to walk in, and some to work in by way of indulgence. Had I not been told I was among 200 insanes, I certainly should not have found it out. All the patients were at liberty, altho' the great heat was rather unfavourable to them, yet all seemed perfectly tranquil — no noise — there was only one, an old woman, who was talking more loudly than the rest; and she was not at all violent. It was a fête day, and they were all very nicely dressed. I only saw two male keepers — the sisters were everywhere, and seemed to be quite revered. The male keepers were sent for in cases of extraordinary violence and their coming, and the going away of the sisters was a punishment, a disgrace so dreaded, as to be of rare occurrence. It really was the most extraordinary sight I ever saw, contrasting strongly with the famous asylum at Venice. I found, on inquiry, that very little medicine was given, and that almost all was done by warm baths. The first, and late Superior of this singular establishment, was a very extraordinary woman, of high family, who, by force of character and manner, gained all the marvellous ascendancy. You will see an interesting notice of her in Southey's work on celebrated women, when it comes out. We had read of the Ordonnances of Bordeaux, but knew nothing of the wondrous events of the three memorable days till our arrival at Pau by Auch, and Tarbes on the 2nd August, where we were detained a fortnight waiting to know what to do. In fact, beautiful as is the situation of the place, we began to be impatient to be off. There were upwards of seventy English families there last winter; and one might have taken it for an English colony. We went over to the little watering places of Eauxbonnes and Eauxchaudes, and were delighted with the scenery. We then went to St Sauveur where we had a capital house, and, having plate, and a good cook with us, settled ourselves most comfortably for three weeks. Here we had horses and guides, and made excursions. St S — is about three quarters of a mile from Luz (the pretty little capital of a little mountain district), and magnificently, beautifully situated at the entrance of the Gap of Gavarnie, the last village on the French frontier, communicating with Spain by the port or pass (all the mountain passes of the Pyrenees are called ports) de Gavarnie, a mule road, and by the far-famed Brêche de Roland, practicable only by *hardy* pedestrians. We all went to Gavarnie — those of our party little accustomed (to) terrific mountain roads in *chaises à porteurs* (a common straw-bottomed light arm-chair with an oil-case top to it, carried like a sedan chair by two men) the gentlemen and myself on horseback. All the world goes to see the cirque, and cascade de Gavarnie. The latter is the highest known, having a fall of 1,266 feet French or upwards of 1,870 feet English, rising from the glacier at the top of the cirque, and falling down the perpendicular face of this *immense* amphitheatre. It would be difficult to give you an idea of this scene. Imagine an amphitheatre above two miles in circumference, and above three hundred yards high in the glacier, and then backed by the *marboré*, an immense wall of marble rock from which rise what are called the *tours des marboré*, and Mont Perdu, and at the other end is cut the marvellous Brêche de Roland, cut at one stroke of his famous durandal (as witness Ariosto), and which, tho' above a hundred yards wide and above a hundred yards deep, does indeed look like a mere gash. In about two hours hardish climbing up the rock, we (of course I do not include the *chaise à porteurs* party) got to the first glacier, so steep that, in spite of iron cramps strapped round our feet, and long iron pointed sticks in our hands to hold by, it was with some difficulty we got up it. In the next glacier, still worse than the other, one of the guides with an axe cut little steps for himself and the rest of us, that we could just stick our toes into, and, one after another, we all got safe over. There was then merely a ravine of snow between us and the Brêche. Getting to the bottom did not give us much trouble — my foot slipped, I found myself sitting instead of standing, and, in this way, glided down so nicely they all thought I had done it on purpose. Well there was no escape near where I was. The view from the Brêche, looking down on France on one side and Spain on the other, on mountains heaped on mountains, is widely magnificent.

The walls of rock on each side may be perhaps twenty yards thick yet being above a hundred yards high, looked so thin, one could hardly feel secure that the first gust of wind would not tumble them upon us. It was too cold to loiter long, and we descended as we could down a chaos of huge torn off fragments into a valley of white marble rock and shiggle with merely little scattered patches of green here and there, yet full of fat beautiful sheep. At three the next morning we were off by candlelight, and at eight had reached the summit of Mt Perdu. The view was indescribably magnificent, tho' fog hung over the distant plains of Spain, and rather blocked up the deep vallies of France. It was not, however, for the view that I had gone up — it was to try the effect of the air at so great an elevation ... [3]

We returned by the Port de Gavarnie, and then by a circuitous mountain path to St Sauveur. We saw Barèges, and Cauteretz, and all the lions thereabouts. I crossed the Tourmolet of Bagnères, Mt Bigorre and back, after which we all spent some time there and liked it less than any place in the Pyrenees. It is neither enough in the mountains, nor enough out of them, and is the very watering-pot of the whole country. From Bagnères to Luchon, (far the prettier, pleasanter Bagnères of the two), I rode over the mountains, back to B(agnères de B(igorre) and thence by the fine valley of the Neste to St Bertrand, (a curious old town founded by Pompey), St Bèat, and along the Spanish Valeurs d'Arran (Val d'Aran) to Viella, saw the two sources of the Garonne, and by the terrible Maladetta to Venasquez (Benasque), where I slept two nights, and where the people delighted at my caring so little either for guerillas or carabinier, overwhelmed me with kindness, I never was so fêted in my life, and more than half promised to see them again. Of course, I do not mean to set up the Pyrenees against the Alps — they have two or three hundred thousand feet less of elevation; and the greater southern latitude thaws off their snowy caps, and the glaciers, which are of small extent, lie only on the northern declivities. It is

---

[3] The description omitted here is almost the same as that in the letter dated September 13 1830. *see* p. 132

a magnificent range of mountain, inhabited by a peasantry to me more interesting than the Swiss and whose legends have had an Ariosto to sing them. On the French side all is pasture, with here and there little terrassed up plots of corn ground, that look like hanging gardens — or covered with tall box. There is very little wood, the forests having been destroyed to get rid of the bears and wolves. The latter, however, are still very troublesome in winter, and come down at night even into the streets of Luz. On the Spanish side, the forests of pine and beech are magnificent; but they are impassable during the whole winter; and, from Mt Perdu down to Torla (sixteen or eighteen miles), there is only one human habitation, a shepherd's hut, and that occupied only during the summer. From Bagnères de Luchon we went to Toulouse, thence to Narbonne, Montpellier, Nîmes, Arles, Marseilles and Toulon to Hières, where we spent a week, and were delighted with the climate and scenery. We returned by Marseilles, and Avignon, and the Rhone to Lyons where we spent two or three days. I went to Cette and Vaucluse, the latter a very pretty picturesque village, that might as well deserve the praise bestowed on it as most places that have been praised so much. As a river, taking it from source to Embonchure, I do not think the Rhone to be compared with the Rhine. I have not paper to make any remark upon the antiquities of the south of France; but those of Nismes are magnificent. Mrs Norcliffe will tell you how much they have been taken care of, and how much money has been judiciously spent upon them of late. No wonder the honey of Narbonne is so celebrated, and that of the whole of the south is so good — the white hills are covered with aromatics; and not Arabia's spicy gale can be more fragrant than the light breeze that wafts the shores of the Mediterranean. The clear blue sky — the scented air was delightful; but, save in the dark green orange-gardens of Hières, there was a glare that blinded me. All is too white — the rosemary, lavendar, thyme that cover the mountains are hoary as the limestone itself; and the olive is little better. The vines are kept very low; and the vineyards at the end of September, are merely a white ground spotted with yellow. But I can say no more; nor is it necessary to add more than that I had a most agreeable tour ... Remember me very kindly to my friends in the Minster Yard, and in Micklegate, and believe me, my dear Mr and Mrs Duffin, ever very affectionately and faithfully yours, A.L. -

Willm Duffin, Esq
   Micklegate, York,
      Angleterre.

12

ENGLAND (WITH A DUTCH INTERLUDE)

1831

On her arrival in England Miss Lister accepted Lady Stuart's invitation to The Lodge, Richmond Park, where she found her friend, Vere Hobart, seriously ill. She wrote immediately to Lady Stuart de Rothesay informing her of this, and mentioning their plan of spending the winter in Italy if old Lady Stuart could be left alone; she then continued as follows:-

We had really a pleasant journey to Calais without either dust or rain tho' Fahrenheit was at 96° in the sun outside the carriage on Tuesday — fifteen hours from Calais to London — the fog so thick we were obliged to cast anchor two or three times. I cannot resist telling you the fate of the shawl. Lady Mexborough's inadvertently saying, 'It would make a pretty gown' was not thrown away; and I am grateful to her for thus saving the character of my taste. This hair-breadth 'scape and the bad cut of a skirt will throw me into the arms of Victorine who, I hope, will rule more ably the destinies of my toilette. You will remember my mentioning a bookseller who, for ready money, furnishes books at 25 p.c. below the published prices in the sheets — something less if in boards — the address is Mr George Stockley, No 18 Bolingbroke Row, Walworth Road. I am quite delighted with the Lodge. What a dear, beautiful, lovely little spot. I shall not at all like London again but it will only be for tomorrow night, as we are to be at Leamington on Wednesday. I hope you will *one day* remember me and St Sauveur. Believe me, dear Lady Stuart, very truly yours,

A. Lister.

Richmond Park. June 8 (1831).

My dear Miss Lister, I have nothing in the world to tell you, (which you will say is a promising commencement to my letter) but you desired and I promised to write, so you must take the consequences, and I dare not let any more time slip, lest you should visit and quit the *direction* before my unhappy epistle arrives. First and foremost come the natural wants of the body, and I must say how delicious *we* found your Marseilles figs, the treasure of a box arrived the evening after you left us, and the dear little acorn safe and dry and unsticky, and as sweet to my nose as the figs to my palate. Many of our friends who have since dined with us have praised them as much as we — in short, I marvel much at your parting with them so easily, you see how *I* would have acted in similar circumstances — gobbled them up, to be sure. I am just as well as when you were here . . . I am often tired and languid . . . Believe me very affectionately yours,

V. Hobart.

Micklegate, York. Sunday evening. 26 June 1831.

I know you will be glad, my dear aunt, to hear how I arrived here, and what sort of journey I had after the rainy day I conclude it would be at Shibden yesterday. I did not see Mr Parker, he had sprained his ankle, and was laid up in bed. I signed the notices, and told Mr Adam to send a regular notice to Mr Emmett about the brook — went to the bank, got what was necessary, took up Cameron, and off from Halifax at ten minutes before two. Hazy, and a little drizzling rain to Bradford, from the latter place to York, where I arrived at five minutes before eight, *rain*, more or less, the whole way. I found the Duffins quite well, and very glad to see me. They made many inquiries after you, and beg their best regards. In passing along I could not help observing on the comparatively fine clear air of Halifax. Never in my life did I see a more smoky place than

Bradford. I really think it beats Burnley which we remember of old. The great long chimneys are doubled, I think, in number, within these two or three years — the same may be said of Leeds. I begin to consider Halifax one of the cleanest and most comely of manufacturing towns ... Today we have been twice at church and have walked towards Acomb. The Yorkes are gone to Scarbro' which I am sorry for. Mrs Best called this morning between the churches. I shall make calls tomorrow, and will see Horner if I can. Will you tell Macdonald, I think she would find one of the carriage towels left behind in one of the little top drawers. I forgot to pay her eight and something for my three weeks washing — perhaps you had better give her the eight shillings and I will pay the pence on my return. I hope Mallinson would quite understand about his job in the back room — there is to be a brick wall of a brick-length in breadth built across the room from the pillar — a new window of two lights nineteen inches wide each, and to open sashwise, and a door to communicate with your room, and the back room, or that part of it taken in, is to be lowered as much as it can conveniently, six or eight inches at least, and is to have a boarded floor. Of course, the door will be all ready to put up (painted first coat) before the door is broken into your room, and, if all is well managed, I do hope you will run no risk of getting cold, and that you will not be much inconvenienced. Let them begin this part of the job earlyish in the morning, and all may be pulled down and made up again by night. I trust we shall have a little dry weather by and by, and you will have less pain ... I shall send for Myers tomorrow about the carriage, and shall make up my mind as well as I can about the other and more important business about which you know I shall be anxious till it is done. I hear Lady Gordon is anxious to know when and where she can see me. V(ere) has told her at the Lodge or in Hertford Street the end of August. You will be glad to hear I can leave Cameron with a friend of hers here when I please, and for as long as I please, in comfort, so that I need have no trouble on this score. I think Lady G — has some plan or other. It would not surprise me at all if we make up something together. Write or not just as you feel inclined. You shall hear from me again the moment I have fixed about Langton ... A.L. -

Micklegate, York. Sunday 3 July 1831.

151

I am determined, my dear aunt, always to take no news for good news, and am therefore contented about you at present. I trust that you have got your teeth again, and that they are well done ... I went with Mr and Mrs Duffin on Friday to see poor Eliza. I *think* she knew me, tho' she would not appear to do so. We were with her half an hour and it was really to me the most melancholy half hour I have passed since seeing her last. She was not in very good humour, yet quiet — the whole of her conversation was incoherent. She was very neat and clean, which is, I understand, a thing of no small difficulty from the excessive dirtyness of her habits. I thought her looking exceedingly well, but aged a little from the circumstances of her gums beginning rather to leave her teeth. You are aware that Miss Wilson has been her *personal* guardian since the death of Lady Crawford. A great many of the people I know are out of York, at Scarbro' or elsewhere, among the rest of the Yorkes ... Mrs Henry Belcombe is just returned from Scarbro' and I have promised to breakfast with her tomorrow. Of the other family none but Mr and Mrs Belcombe at home, and in the midst of the bustle of painting and papering or whitewashing the whole house, that no visiting is possible. I wonder how you get on with the back room. Surely it is taken in, and plastered by this time ... I am to be at Langton to dinner on Thursday, and have promised to spend at least a fortnight there. After that they expect me at Croft, and perhaps I shall go for a few days, that probably enough it will be almost August before my getting back to Shibden. The repairs to the carriage are so considerable, they will not be done till the second of that month. In the mean time, Myers lends me a carriage gratis for all I have to do. I have employed him again, because he has behaved as well in the business as he could, and because it is, after all, most convenient to me that the doer of the job should mend it ... Whether I go to Leamington or not, I cannot be off before the first or perhaps second week in August. The carriage is to be done on the 2nd, it is to be new painted, have new springs and wheels, and will, I hope, be better than it ever was before. Wm Milne does not seem to be much better for Leamington ... As I shall be at Langton on Thursday, do take care that Mr Briggs is told not to direct to me here but to Mrs Norcliffe's, Langton Hall, Malton, which address I wish him to give to Messrs. Rawson. I met Mr Rawson (Christopher) here the other day ... A.L. -

Micklegate, (York). Thursday 7 July 1831.

I have this moment, my dear aunt, received your letter, and, being on the point of being off to Langton in half an hour, have really only time to say how happy I am to hear my father is better. I hope, and trust, the weakness he complains of is merely owing to the excessive heat of the weather, and that, even without medicine, he will be quite recovered in a day or two. Of course, if he is not, I shall hear from you soon again. I am, at all rates, delighted to flatter myself that you yourself are better than when I left you. I am sorry to find the back room so much below the level of your room. I think you had better have the fireplace made — £2 is but a small additional expense. But the time of five weeks instead of days is fearful. Do pray tell Mallinson he must begin the job as soon as he can, and stick to it, that is not leave it on any pretense whatever till it is done . . . A.L. -

Draft letter from Anne Lister to Mr Lawton, Proctor, York, concerning her will.

Micklegate. Thursday 7 July 1831.

Sir,

It is so desirable to keep the will as clear as possible, perhaps it will be best to give the annuity as well as the legacies by codicil. I am anxious to provide that the mansion house (Shibden Hall) should not be let but kept in good and sufficient repair and occupied for this purpose by such servants as the executors should think fit. The executors should also have a discretionary power to make what allowance they think fit, but not at any time exceeding £300 a year, for the education of the heir apparent to the property. I wish to bar the opening of any new coal mines or stone quarries and the selling any privileges respecting the loosing or getting any beds or veins of coal not belonging to the estate and to bar the cutting down of all timber, except such as in the estimation of an experienced woodman it may be necessary to remove for the good growth of the rest. Instead of leaving the remainder to the heir at law of my late uncle James Lister, I particularly wish it to (be) left to the heir at law of my great grandfather, James L(ister) of Shibden Hall.

Tho' I have only added to the length and difficulty of the
business, but feel confident that you will manage it with all the
skill and care required, and am, Sir, Yours &c.

Letter from Anne Lister, dated from Langton Hall, (Malton),
24 July 1831, to her aunt at Shibden Hall.

... I think of being off from here on Thursday, shall leave
Cameron in York, and try to get all done I have to do in time
to be off, if I can get a place for myself and one for George,
in the night mail. If I can manage this, I shall be with you to
breakfast on Friday morning — if not, I shall take the next mail
which has room enough to spare. I shall not attempt to fill my
letter with what I can communicate much better by word of
mouth, and shall therefore say nothing of plans of any sort ...
Mrs Norcliffe does not take the *Leeds Intelligencer*, but the *Courier*
has informed us about Stocks, and it really does seem probable
that he will not get reinstated. I see the canvas has begun for
Mr Wm Lascelles and Mr Fawkes. I return, without waiting
for the carriage, because one is never sure of things being done
to the day, and I have excused myself from my visit to Croft
because I am really anxious to see how my father is, and get
something done of home-affairs. We expect all the Marshes,
papa and mama, one daughter, and three sons and two servants
to dinner tomorrow, to stay till Wednesday. But for this I should
have been off a day sooner. We have four Croft Daltons (three
girls and Charles) here, and are a very agreeable party. You
must read me my letter on return, and that will remind me to
tell you at once all I have to say ... A.L. -

York. Monday evening, 1 August 1831.

My dear aunt,

You will not expect to hear from me again, but will be
surprised, perhaps, to find that Mariana is to be my companion.
It has just been arranged for us to make a little tour together
for a fortnight or three weeks. I did not like to go off without
just taking a peep at you; but do tell Marian not to put herself
at all out of her way in making any particular arrangements
for us, as we shall not arrive till between seven and eight

tomorrow evening, and shall be off the next day. I will explain all when we meet. We shall only have George with us; and M — will share my room, and give no trouble. If we might have a little soup, and a mutton chop for M — and a pudding for me at eight, we should have all we want. I am anxious to see how you and my father are, and then I shall be satisfied till my next return, which will be as soon as M — and I have made our little tour. We are to be off from here at half past one tomorrow, or one if we can ... A.L. -

HOLLAND

The 'little tour' referred to was a trip to Holland which the following letter, begun by Anne Lister, and continued by her companion Mrs Mariana Lawton, describes.

Rotterdam. Tuesday 9 August 1831.

You will be glad, my dear aunt, to hear of our safe arrival here. We were off from Shibden about four, as you would hear from John, and, with the exception of a couple of hours' halt at Doncaster for breakfast, and to wait the Edinburgh mail which took us as far as Huntingdon, never stopt till we reached Cambridge (one hundred and sixty miles), about one in the morning of Friday, pretty well for one day's journey. We remained there seeing the sights of the place till about three in the afternoon, and then went to Ipswich where we slept, and were off by the packet from Harwich the next morning, Saturday — or rather at noon when we weighed anchor. It was rather a disappointment to us to find we were not on board a steamer, and that the length of our passage was consequently uncertain. We were thirty hours, and then put on shore in a boat. The accommodations of the little town of Helvoetsluys are not particularly good, but we were glad enough to lay our heads down quietly. Yesterday we came here by the Briel, over land, with the exception of crossing the Maes twice. Everything was (here Miss Lister broke off and her friend continued) something, I suppose, my dear aunt, but as Anne has her journal to write she has given me the pen, I must therefore leave you in the dark respecting the end of her sentence and tell my own story. I am not so surprised with the appearance of the people of Holland

155

as I expected to be, in feature they very much resemble the English, and their dress for the most part, at least the effect, is pretty much the same, except that they seldom wear bonnets. All their shoes are without hind quarters. The very lowest class have necklaces of some kind, and either earrings or ornaments fastened in some way to hang over the temples. The Inn we were at at Helvoet was a very poor one, but the landlord's sister had diamond earrings on, and a handsome coral necklace of three rows, with a clasp of the same fastened in front. The roads are excellent, paved with small brick on the top of the artificial mound raised to prevent the water gaining admission into the plains, there is just room for two carriages to pass and on each side are rows of willow trees that look half drowned. The country is an unbroken flat, looking like an immense marsh with drains to let off the water. There are many substantial looking farm houses, but all have a moat around them of what looks *very like* stagnant water. The towns thro' which we have passed are beautifully clean and neat, you might eat off the streets which for the most part have canals running thro' them and trees on each side. We arrived here at a quarter past four yesterday, and joined the party at the table d'hôte, the dinner having just been served up. The party were chiefly English. We had a capital dinner, plenty of vegetables and a handsome dessert. Our apartment resembles those in France, two beds in the room, the windows are enormously large, the room twenty-seven feet by twenty-one, and twenty feet high. The situation beautiful, it is called the Boum-quay, and looks on the splendid river Maes, bordered with magnificent elms. I can give you no idea of the town, it is most extraordinary and not to be imagined. Canals are cut from the river through every part of the city, and the sides are mostly planted with tall trees, the houses are immensely high, and in consequence of being built on piles to preserve the foundations that are chiefly out of the perpendicular and look as if they were going to tumble upon you. Nearly all the houses have looking glasses projecting from each side of the windows that those within may see all that passes without. One street is three miles long, it divides the old and new town, each of which are composed of innumerable islands, so that one sees water and bridges in almost every street; but as the tide enters twice a day, the water is very pure, and the place healthy. Yet we should both be sorry to live in Holland, the climate is soft and damp, and everything feels clammy, if not wet, as for beds we fancy we have had no dry one since we landed. We are off today to the Hague. Little seems known of politics, no one appears to trouble their heads on the subject, and as we are assured there is no danger for us, we shall see what we intended of Holland, and return to England the end of next week, going up the Rhine seems out of the question. Anne is quite well, and joins me in love to all at Shibden,

believe me, my dear aunt,

Yours affectionately,
M.P. Lawton.

Peterborough. Saturday 20 August 1831.

... I hope you got the letter Mariana finished for me, from Rotterdam. From there we went to the Hague, Leyden, Haarlem, Amsterdam, Utrecht, and thence back to Rotterdam where we embarked on Tuesday afternoon, and reached London about half past four on Wednesday afternoon. We made haste to dress and dine, and then went to the King's theatre (the opera house) to hear Paganini whose wondrous fiddling on one string surprised and kept us awake in spite of a rather restless night the night before on board the steamer. Yet strange to say, neither M -nor I was sick at all. We were off from London before six on Thursday morning, and dined at Norwich before nine in the evening. We slept at Newmarket last night, breakfasted this morning at Ely, and arrived here at three this afternoon. We have had a most agreeable, interesting little tour. Mariana bids me give her best love, and say, she played the organ at Haarlem, and went up 450 steps to look down upon fifty walled towns from the church steeple at Utrecht. We are both glad to have visited Holland of which we have never seen the like anywhere else till today, between Ely and here, twenty miles of road which, for canals and dykes, may be called English Holland. I thought of Mrs Hunter while listening to the organ at Haarlem, which is really finer than ever our imagination had portrayed. The trumpet stop astonished us most. We liked the town, too, exceedingly — better than any place we saw in Holland till our arrival at Utrecht which has the character of being the most beautiful city in Holland next to the Hague. Our excursions from Amsterdam, to see Peter the Great's cottage at Saardam,

157

and the singularly and beautifully grotesque village of Brock, delighted us. And to return to home sights, we were much pleased with Norwich, and particularly comfortable there — the best bread and butter I have ever tasted, save in Lombardy. The three cathedrals of Norwich, Ely and here, have interested us exceedingly. They are all under repair, this one here is all but completed, and the prettiest, neatest church imaginable. We are impatient to see Lincoln. Up to this moment, no ecclesiastical building I have ever seen equals York cathedral. My best love to my father and Marian. I have only time to add, ever, my dear aunt, very affectionately yours, A.L. -

ENGLISH TRAVELS

At this period Miss Lister was considering accompanying Lady Duff Gordon to Spain. The latter had business to transact at Cadiz and desired Miss Lister, with her 'far better head', to take charge of her affairs there. Miss Lister was quite agreeable, but apparently the journey proved unnecessary, as it was not undertaken. In reply to one of Miss Lister's business-like letters, Lady Gordon remarked:- 'Your letter is just like yourself, sensible, agreeable, and to the purpose'.

Still another plan was to winter in Italy with her friend, Vere Hobart, whose health was delicate, but on its being considered unwise for Miss Hobart to go abroad, it was finally decided that they should spend a few months at Hastings. In the mean time, Miss Lister seemed unable to settle down at home, and therefore spent the next few weeks in travelling in the south of England.

In the next letter Miss Lister describes her first journey by train, on the recently opened Liverpool to Manchester line. Possibly Miss Lister senior's apprehensions concerning the projected Manchester to Leeds railway were caused by her interest in the Calder and Hebble Navigation, in which concern she was a shareholder, and which might suffer if a new railway line were opened. The letter dated September 30 contains a reference to the Reform Bill.

London, 26 Dover Street. Thursday 15 September 1831.

You will easily imagine, my dear aunt, that I have been in hurry and bustle every since leaving you. Macdonald saw us off from the White Lion. We were at Manchester at eight. Off the next morning at six thirty. Were in Liverpool quarter of an hour, and then back at M — at twelve, having had no time to breakfast, it was half past one before we could get off again. You would hear, I think, from Mrs Sowden, that she had sat next to me in the omnibus out of Liverpool to the steam carriage station. I asked her to call, and let you know. It was impossible not to be surprised, and gratified at the steam expedition. I would not have missed it on any account. We went twenty miles an hour, but so comfortably and steadily, one might have been writing, if one chose it, all the way. Were there no roads but railroads, *you might travel all over. However, you will not for all this grieve much to hear, that it was confidently said in Manchester, that the M — and Leeds railroad was given up.* Great doubts whether it would pay; and the people interested had resolved to relinquish the trial. You may therefore set your mind at ease about the C(alder) & H(ebble) navigation. Good news, you must own, sometimes — that is, not *always* bad. Not being able to get off from Manchester before one thirty, I was obliged to travel all night, or could not have arrived on Tuesday at five. The Lawtons at Warren's, but I, not daring to count upon them, had written on Sunday night from Manchester for rooms here, where I was exceedingly comfortable. Lady G(ordon) had called twice before my arrival, and she and Sir Alexander came, and sat with me above an hour, and then came M(ariana) and staid till eleven . . . I took leave of M(ariana) last night, for tho' they will be back tonight, and stay till Saturday, I shall be all the while at the Lodge. I shall be there a week. Nothing can have been kinder than both the Ladies S(tuart). Lady S(tuart) de R(othesay) leaves London today for their place in Hampshire; she has been staying at Lord Harwick's. I luncheoned with them all, yesterday; and never people more civil, and kind, and attentive. Lady S(tuart) de R(othesay) has provided me with, or at least put me in the way of getting, a courier that I think will exactly suit me. I really thank heaven for all my good luck. No merit of mine — I certainly do not deserve it. I see far better people than I sticking fast where I get on glibly. Lady Gordon was delighted to see me — wanted me very much to go to her at Brighton, and made me promise always to write and give her timely notice of what I was about, as she had several plans in view. In fact, my dear aunt, you do not need have a moment's uneasyness about me — only take care of yourself, and let me have good accounts of you, and I shall have all I want ... I went to Hammersleys yesterday. His civility and even kindness surprised me — he said — he should not mind my any time overdrawing my account £100 — they had known me so long — they had perfect confidence, and would do anything they could for me. Mr Lawton happened to be with me, and seemed not a little surprised too. Mr Hammersley put me into the way of having a letter of credit to any amount I could wish, without inconveniencing myself; and, as he said, a large credit might sometimes be of use. I am thinking of it — one needs not spend the more. I am on the point of being off to the Lodge and have written in a great hurry ... A.L. -

Poole, Dorsetshire. Friday evening 30 September 1831.

You will wonder, my dear aunt, at my date. I myself had no thought of it when I wrote to you last, from Richmond Park. I did not, after all, get off from there till this day week, and then, instead of going back to London, made up my mind to accept Lady S(tuart) de R(othesay)'s very kind invitation to High Cliff, and spent four days and a half with her there, left her on Wednesday, to see Swanage, a beautiful little bay and sea bathing place one and twenty miles from here, where I slept that night. Yesterday saw Corfe Castle and Lulworth Cove, and slept at Wareham, and today am arrived here, lucky not to have been stopt for want of horses, for the whole country is in a ferment; and the contest between Lord Ashley in the tory interest, and Mr Ponsonby a reformer, will be hard fought. Good hopes for Ashley — *the bill* seems to have lost friends in the country, tho' the shew of hands was to be in favour of Ponsonby; for all the unemployed labourers, and all the scamps, they said, of Wareham, had been hired to go to Dorchester for the reformer. Tomorrow, I mean to go to Brownsea Island, shall sleep here, go to church here on Sunday morning, and then return to High Cliff to dinner and stay all night. Monday I talk of sleeping at Lymington. Whether I shall cross from here or from Southampton to the Isle of Wight, depends upon weather and other uncertain circumstances. I shall take Portsmouth in my return, and have just been writing to say, I hoped I should see Lady S(tuart) and Miss H(obart), in passing, (Richmond Park), on Monday-week. After all it is probable that Miss H(obart) and I may spend the winter together somewhere or other. She begged till the 20th of next month, and, not caring to be dawdling about either at the Lodge, or in London so long as this, I came down to High Cliff, and determined on the little further tour made, and to be made. I have enjoyed it exceedingly so far. I slept at Winchester on my way down, and was much interested in the fine old cathedral. High Cliff is a charming place, four miles from Christchurch, Hants. The church at Christchurch is a large, cathedral-like, fine remain of one of the oldest and most celebrated monasteries in England. Swanage is a little recluse village brought into vogue by Mr Moreton Pitt to whom it chiefly belongs. He has enlarged the old manor house, and fitted it up as an excellent hotel which, as well as several nice lodging houses, is now always full of good company during the sea bathing season. It is from the immediate neighbourhood of this village that the famous Purbeck paving stone used to be sent to London; but, spoilt by prosperity, they got the stone up to such a price, that Yorkshire stepped in upon them, and the market is now almost wholly transferred from the one to the other. The high cliffs towards the west shew the curious position of the stone, which cliffs, the stone lying in the strata of clay, have a ribbon-like appearance singularly striking. The hill, a down, above the village, is studded with quarries worked to different depths. I went down one of the deepest, 110 feet deep. The stone is drawn up a very steep inclined plane by a horse-turned windlass. The seam of stone in the shaft I visited, was only about two and a half to three feet thick, so that there was no standing upright. As I did not choose being sledged down, we went along the deep, bad, difficult, dirty steps on one side, it was hottish work. The ruins of Corfe Castle are very fine. The guide pointed out the very gateway under which Edward the Martyr was stabbed. From here I walked across the hills to Lulworth Castle. The sea views would have been magnificent, but the weather was unfortunately rather hazy — but I was amply repaid for my trouble. The castle is a large solid square of building, with a large round tower at each corner, the whole forming a very large, excellent house. The French royal family rented it of Mr Wild, and did a great deal of good among the poor, and were much liked. They gave something

161

over and above their wages to all employed, and made handsome presents to Mr Wild's family. There is a fine peep of the sea from the castle, through a natural cleft in the cliffs — some goodish forest timber round the castle, then moors in all directions, that Charles X had, at least, plenty of range for shooting — but no wonder the poor duchesse de Berri grew dull. Walked, too, over the moors to Wareham, and think of Cameron's have (having?) chosen and adventured to go with me. She had never walked so far (about fourteen miles) in her life before, and was, of course, sadly tired, but she did very well, and was no worse this morning. I am glad to see so much enterprize — it is a good sign in the present case. Wareham is a nice, neat, little town, sixteen miles from Dorchester, and eighteen from Weymouth. Having seen both the latter, I had no object for going there now. I must see Devonshire one of these days if I live, and Cornwall when a better mineralogist. I was *not* sorry *not* to be on my way to Falmouth for the Cadiz packet. I should have told you that, in our way from Corfe to Lulworth, were the famous pits that furnish the clay of the Staffordshire potteries. A three miles railroad takes it down to the Wareham channel where it is put into Lighters that bring it here (Poole) whence it is shipped or barged for Staffordshire. Poole is a good town and busy port. There are several very rich merchants who have large, handsome-looking houses, and bring their riches in blubber from Newfoundland — they were very successful the last season. It has been raining heavily for the last hour, so that I have had no outgoing duty, and have been writing very comfortably before dinner ...

A.L. -

Richmond Park. Saturday 15 October 1831.

My letter from Poole, my dear aunt, would tell you enough to prepare you for my being unsettled for two or three weeks. I did all I said — went to Brownsea Island, back to High Cliff for two or three days and then (Tuesday evening October 18 1831) by Lymington and Southampton to the Isle of Wight of which I saw all that was worth seeing in three and a half days, and then gave a day to Portsmouth, and a couple of incessantly rainy days sat settling accounts at Chichester, and then, having

162

a fine afternoon for Arundel Castle, made the best of my way to Guildford &c., the next day (last Friday) and dined on that day at the Lodge, and only left there, and arrived here (26 Dover Street) about two, today. I had written four lines all but the two last words (by Lymington) of this page, when some interruption came, and my letter remained unfinished. Quite as well it did so, for I can now tell you something a little more fixed as to my plans for a little while to come. I told you in my last, that Miss H(obart) and I would probably spend the winter together somewhere, but that she had asked me to wait for her till the 20th. We have at last fixed upon Hastings, she not making a point of crossing the water, and I being glad to have a little more time in England; so I have told her, she may count upon having me for three or four months . . . I went to Lymington to see and judge for myself about the pretty cottages people talk so much of. I have been on the look out for a dry air — but the fact is, I have not found one; and I am come back here persuaded more than ever, that the South of England, tho' more mild, is decidedly more humid than the north. I cannot describe to you how deeply I lament over what you tell me about the air at Shibden. I am quite puzzled to know what to do. I am quite persuaded of not having been in one place since leaving you, which would be at all likely to suit you better. I was thinking seriously of asking if you would like to return to Paris; but we had Lord S(tuart) to spend the day and stay all night on Sunday, and what he said, made me think this would be such madness . . .

13

HALIFAX AFFAIRS — PEW RENTS — COAL LEASES — SERVANTS AT SHIBDEN HALL

1832-1833

Hastings. Tuesday January 10 1832.

Sir,

I have just received your letter of the 8th inst. Of the three, Carr, Greenwood, and Pickersgill, I am disposed, tho' I do not know him, to prefer the last; as you are informed, that he is a very industrious man, and would be a likely tenant. Neither Carr, nor Greenwood would live upon the place; and, if we should be sure of the rent, and of neat, good farming from Pickersgill, he would suit much better than anyone who would put servants, or cottagers, or both into the house. But you who are on the spot can judge best; and I shall be satisfied with what you do, immediately upon the matter being settled, I beg you to communicate it to my father, that he may not hear it from anyone, before he has heard it from you. You will, of course, take care to have the lease signed, before giving possession. Do whatever you think necessary and advisable for putting the place into proper, tenantable repair. In your letter on Monday, I shall be obliged to you to send me Washington's measurement of the land, specifying the quantity contained in Bairstow. And I shall be glad to know if anything has been settled with Mr Wilkinson about the water at Lower brea.

I am, Sir, &c., &c.
A. Lister.

Mr James Briggs,
Horton Street,
Halifax.

Hastings. Wednesday 18 January 1832.

I see it was three weeks yesterday, my dear aunt, since I wrote to you — too long; but I was somehow not aware of it . . . It seems to me as if I never knew the hours roll on so fast before. Spring will soon be upon us; and, by that time, I must have some fixed plan, fixed I mean in all its details. It is impossible to calculate now what may, or can be done by then. We are in some apprehension, spite of all the hush-up about it, that the cholera has reached London — if so, and a few days will shew, there will be no telling the consequences. Going to the continent may be impossible under less than a forty days' quarantine; and that is no joke, however anxious one may be. But sufficient till the day is the evil thereof; and I shall leave the subject for the present. I do not much like what you say of yourself. I fear you are suffering much in your limbs. I think of you perpetually and with more anxiety than I can describe. We have little to thank Charles X for. Had he been a wise man, our establishment in Paris needed not have been broken up. It had its comforts and, tho' there might be some things to grumble at, we had perhaps as little reason to be dissatisfied as one generally has in this world. But it is grievous now to see the unsettled state of peoples and governments. Thank you for all your home news — tho' I am sorry for every man's troubles, even Stock's, yet I am glad we are not likely to have him for our member — there seems no doubt that the bill will pass. Were you not shocked at the melancholy end of Col Brereton?[1] I do not want Whitley to line our pew for us; for then the value would never wear out . . . My kindest regards to the Wm Priestleys. I have more than once thought of writing to *her*. She is very good; tell her, I think I shall want her to contrive a neat, but economical little bookcase for you, to stand in the drawing room, like one of hers. I have got about a hundred neat little volumes that I mean to send you. British Essayists, selection from British prose writers, Fielding's and Smollett's works, and the British theatre, besides a large edition of Shakespeare, Sir Walter Scott's border antiquities, and Smith's Italy which will amuse you exceedingly in explanation, as I hope, of my future letters. Do ask Whitley to advise me how to send them down — by water from London, I should think ... A.L. -

Anne Lister, at Hastings, to her aunt at Shibden Hall, 3 February 1832.

... What do you pay for my letters? 1/3? I might ask Lord Skelmersdale[2] to frank for me; but, you know, I never ask even the smallest thing, when I can well enough do without it. Our society might be much enlarged if we chose; but as one from necessity (health), and the other from choice, declines going out in an evening, we are not visiting people, and our *friends* do not multiply beyond measure ... Lord and Lady Skelmersdale and their daughter Miss Wilbraham have been here about a month, and stay two or three weeks longer, excellent people, and a great gain to us ... The Courtenays, too, are still here, except Mr C — gone to attend to his duties in the house of commons. Whether ministers will keep their places long, who can tell — they have more difficulties even about their reform bill, than meets the eye all at once. Spite of what the ministerial papers say, H.M. does not much like it (the bill) at heart. About forty new peers are wanted; but twenty that voted for the last bill have determined to vote against this, *if* there is a new creation, so that sixty new peers are, in fact, wanted; and ministers are rather startled. How it will all end, Heaven knows. I think some of the ministerial papers begin to be a good deal less cock-a-whoop than they were. It seems the queen's illness is rather a thing of convenience. So much company at the palace is not to be borne, in these times — the royal income has been a good deal outrun these two last quarters; and now it is made a rule to invite none but the peers and their children, so that none below honorable (except a few particulars and those holding office of some sort) will be seen at the royal table in future — the *family party* is about thirty. No truth in the hints thrown out

---

[1] Thomas Brereton (1782-1832), Lieut Col committed suicide on January 13 1832, during his trial for neglect of duty during the Reform Riots in Bristol.

Anne Lister's Book-plate

by some of the papers, that her M. is likely to increase the establishment; but there are five nurseries already in the palace — four of Fitzclarences of one sort or other, and that of the princess Louise. The lady of high rank said to have eloped the other day was the young duchess of Richmond — never was there a greater or more unjust scandal — but as she was a Paget, people fancy they may say anything . . . I am sorry the drawing room smokes. Surely not enough to spoil the books — they are gilt-edged — some in crimson, some in green morocco, all well bound — their cheapness tempted me. Whitley would charge a good deal more for the binding than I paid for books and all. What I meant was such a little book-case as Mrs W. P(riestley) has two in her common sitting room. Common shelves neatly put together, painted black, with a narrow yellow edge, or border, or something of that sort. We must think about it. I do not think any of the books so bad to read as a newspaper. It grieves me to hear your eyes are so much worse . . . Tell

McD(onald) I am much obliged to her for taking care of my minerals, and hope that she will put windows and doors open when the weather is good to air my books; and also that she will be so good as keep them sufficiently dusted ... If you ever read novels, do send for *Eugene Aram*. Miss H(obart) and I have just read it, and thought it well done ... I wish you would be so good as send me by the mail the three or four 8vo French books, tours to the Pyrenees, that I left I think in the second or third compartment from the library door (in the library passage). All have thin paper backs (three blue and one yellowish). If *you* could be got up there, you would find them at once ...

Miss Lister senior, in a letter to her niece on February 8, 1832, remarked that Paganini was to perform in Halifax the next evening, and that William Cobbett had lectured twice during the previous week. Regarding postal rates and political affairs she wrote:- I pay 1/1 for your letters. I do not think many would be so scrupulous about asking for the franking a letter, now and then, as you are, as in these days people in general are for all they can get in any way ... Some think ministers will be out, before April 1. The King and Queen are not to be envied. It is said, the Fitzclarences behave very ill to the latter. The hints in the newspaper respecting the increase expected, I daresay no one believes. This is but a stupid letter but I am glad to get it, and the books off this evening, and hope you will receive both safe.

In replying to her aunt's letter, Anne remarked that a change in ministry seemed likely; and she denied the truth of the rumour that the Fitzclarences treated the Queen badly, for they were too fond of her for that. She also mentioned an excursion to Eastbourne which she had made with Miss Hobart, and long walks which she had taken from Hastings, once to Battle Abbey, a distance of eight miles, and another time to Winchelsea, which was nine miles away. In her next letter Miss Lister mentions among other things, the cholera menace.

Hastings. Sunday 19 February 1832.

---

[2] Edward Bootle-Wilbraham (1771-1853), created Baron Skelmersdale, 1828.

My dear aunt,

... Somehow or other, I have not yet had resolution to execute the will made by Lawton the proctor, and that you read over — the thing is, it is not, as I told you at the moment, *exactly* what I intended; but I hardly know how to amend it just now — it would be far better than no will, and I think of executing it, *or* I may have some alterations made in London. If anything happens to me in the mean time, I am satisfied to think, there is a short will properly executed, in the middle drawer of the deal chest in the blue room, leaving everything I have to you. The cholera is decidedly in London, but the panic about it is rather subsiding. The commercial stagnation may perhaps be the worse evil of the two. If I could be off now, I could, by sailing from Dover, land at Calais after only three days quarantine — but I fear this cannot last long, and that, before the middle of April, we shall have no *clean* port to sail from. Amid all this fearful uncertainty, it is impossible to form any plans. All I can say is, you shall hear my intentions as soon as I am able to tell them. I have just engaged an Italian courier who is to come to me some time in April, of which time he is hereafter to have a fortnight's notice. He is little, and slim, but looks quick, and clever, says he will do anything, drive or cook for me, if I like; and I am in better hope, because he lived for seven years with his last master, the honorable Leicester Stanhope, who gives him an excellent character, and says he (Francesco Bado) has a small estate near Genoa. I am certainly better in health than I was at first, but still feel as if the very sight of my books in Paris would do me good. I wish those I have here were safe with you ... Do ask my father to send John to see about Lower brea wood and Tilly holm railing being all properly mended up. And let the Cunnery fences against the wood, and trough of Bolland wood fences, and the fence between Jonathan Mallinson's holm and Lower brea wood be well looked to. John can easily look round and see what is wanted ... I know now what we shall all say to a 7 ½ and 10 p.c. property tax. Nothing has been said about it here ... A.L. -

Hastings. Friday March 23 1832.

I am always delighted to hear from you, my dear aunt, tell me what you may. Never mind how many reasons McDonald has for leaving you — the reason given, health, is good — think not of more. Five pounds (£5) will certainly be quite enough to allow for her journey, considering that the following is a copy of the account she gave of the expenses of her journey on arriving

'Coach fare from Edinburgh to Newcastle 30/-
Guard and Coachman 4/3
Breakfast on the road 1/6
Expenses at Newcastle, Bed and chambermaid 1/6,
Breakfast 1/6
Coach fare from Newcastle to Leeds 22/-
Guard and Coachman 1/-
Porter 6d.
Expenses all night at Leeds 2/9, Porter 6d.
Coach fare from Leeds to Halifax 1/-
Guard and Coachman 1/-
Altogether equal to £3/10/6.'

All I am anxious about is, for you to get some one to suit you ... You are not difficult to suit, because you neither require skill in mantua-making, or hair-dressing. McD-'s cleverness, in the lady's-maid-way, is not so great, as to leave you no hope of meeting with the like again — her forte is in nursing and care. And surely our parish is not deficient in these joined to respectability and a comfortable degree of proper manners. 'An affected, self-opinionated, doubting, contradicting person' requires a *monstrous deal* to make up for so much of the disagreeable. Be of good cheer, my dear aunt. You make me think you are not likely to be a loser by the change ... Never mind *a little obliging* vulgarity — things will mend by and by ... You are very very good about money matters. Indeed, indeed, my dear aunt, I never think of all you have done, without far more affectionate gratitude than I have ever been able to express. And as to the *interpretation* of all my thoughts, words, and actions, I often say to Miss H(obart), you are the only kind and reasonable person I have to count upon ...

J.L. & B. Hammond, in *The Age of the Chartists*, call attention to the fact that in the early nineteenth century, when only a small proportion of church seats were free, some people in Halifax owned pews in more than one church. Anne Lister not only owned several pews in different churches, but it was evidently her practice to let the pews she did not require at a good rent. This is clear from the following letters.

To Mr James Briggs
    or J. Lister, Esq.

Sirs,

When I took the Pew from you (which I at present occupy) the rent was £1.11.6 per annum but in consequence of their becoming scarce it was advanced to £3.13.6., they are now again to be had upon much lower terms. (I am of opinion they are now lower than they were when I took this.)

The present is to say, I will either give up possession or I will give you the original rent, you will oblige me by a reply.

       I remain Sirs Your mo. obed, Servant
George Whiteley.

                  Halifax. June 29 1832.

Madam,

I am favoured with your note and will accept the Pew at the Rent proposed namely two pounds per annum payable as before (although I consider it high).

I have to apologize for my last note being addressed wrong but being ignorant who was the owner will account for its being so.

       I am Madam Your mo. obed. Servant
George Whiteley.

              Windhill Lane. July 2 1832.

Mrs Christopher Rawson's comp(limen)ts to Miss Lister and she returns the keys belonging to the pew Miss Walker occupied. They were sent a week ago to Mr James Briggs, and they were only returned yesterday.

Mrs Rawson will feel obliged if Miss Lister would inform her how much Miss Walker is indebted for the pew.

West Grove, Thursday morning (September 20 1832).

On January 8 Miss Lister wrote:-I hear Mr Whitley has lined his pew in the new Church. I would rather pay him what he has laid out, and fix the rent accordingly.

To Anne Lister, at Shibden Hall.

Madam,

I have the pleasure to inform you that the Godley Lane Road com(missione)rs will meet you on Monday next at ten o'clock to settle the matter with you as to the temporary road. The committee are Mr Stocks, Mr Wm Emmet, & Mr John Hodgson. The footpath is considered quite unnecessary, and Mr Stocks says that it was at first agreed that the old road should be given up to you, as also the land adjoining which belongs to the com(missione)rs. The fence I fear that they will not make. The committee will also take into consideration the planting of the embankment, which I think they will not object to but will probably require some agreement. For your government I am sure that you will excuse my saying that I could observe Mr Stocks would be very favorable to you, and that anything stated by Mr William Emmet may be fully relied upon. In haste I have the honor to remain,

Madam,

Your faithful servant
Rob. Parker.

Halifax. July 9 1832.

Letter from Mrs Ann Norcliffe, dated from Langton Hall, near Malton, July 12 1832 to Anne Lister, at Shibden Hall.

. . . I wish I could send you a good account of the cholera at York. The last account was yesterday when there were only seven new cases, but it now attacks a more respectable set of people. Bellerby the bookseller's wife, Shepherd the Librarian's, and Miss Robinson the school mistress's daughter, Wolstenholme the spirit merchant, the wife of one of the choristers at the minster, and the mother of one of the singing boys are amongst the 127 already dead in it. People are afraid to venture to York, the Musical Festival is postponed and the assizes are put off. The Duffins very wisely do not return to York yet. We passed a very pleasant week at Scarborough . . . They have so far been most fortunate in never having one case of cholera, and their alarm of it is very great. A vessel appeared as if intending to enter the harbour with the yellow flag at the mast head, a sign of a corpse, or at least sick people were on board, however they were not suffered to come nearer the shore, and not even allowed to wait for high water, but were towed out by a steam packet to the hospital ship off the Humber. They only left Hull on Wednesday, this was Friday and one was dead, and other two died before they reached the hospital . . . I condole with you on the deficiency in the Revenue. What sort of an opinion will they have of our abilities, or what sort of a figure will Lord Durham cut amongst the foreign Diplomatists — they say they have only to put him in a passion (no difficult matter) to get out all his secrets . . .

THE HALIFAX ELECTION. 1832

With the passing of the Reform Bill in 1832, Halifax became entitled to two members of Parliament and at the first election in December of that year the candidates were Michael Stocks (Radical), the Hon. James Stuart Wortley (3rd son of Lord Wharncliffe), (Tory), Charles Wood of Doncaster (later Lord Halifax) (Whig), and Rawdon Briggs (Whig). Anne Lister was a strong Tory, supporting (financially and in other ways) the candidature of James Stuart Wortley, the nephew of her friend Lady Stuart, of Richmond Park. In the letters of this period there are several references to the elections; on November 16 1832 Lady Stuart wrote:- I wrote to my nephew, James Wortley, the other day, and said I had pleasure in hearing he was likely to succeed at Halifax; asked him if he was acquainted with you; I was sure you wished him well. Indeed, dear Miss Lister, I feel I hardly need to ask of you to interest yourself for him, which I now do, particularly as he seems ignorant of your good wishes for him.

And on November 20 she wrote:- I had a note the other day from James Wortley to express strongly how much he is obliged for your good wishes, and hopes when he returns to make himself known to you. He seems to flatter himself he shall succeed.

In those pre-vote-by-ballot days it was easy for propertied people to influence the votes of their tenants and Miss Lister made no secret of the fact that she expected her tenants to vote as she wished. A few extracts from her diary illustrate the corruption in political affairs at this time.

30 July 1832 . . . had John Bottomley. Sent for him to get his vote for Mr Wortley. He had signed, he said, for Lord Grey and Milton but I told him the latter would not come forward that he, Bottomley, was therefore at liberty and must give me his vote which he therefore did.

11 December 1832 Had J(ohn B)ottomley), having sent for him to tell him to vote for Wortley tomorrow. Had a quarter hour's talk. He promised to vote for him . . . They had all been at him and some said they would not employ him again if he would not vote their way, but he told them how I wanted him to vote, and seeming to care nothing about it, but that he thought he ought to oblige me. It is quite useless to leave such men as he uninfluenced. He knows nothing and cares nothing about it, and is literally best satisfied with the idea of pleasing somebody he knows.

12 December 1832 Had Throp — if I could get him his shop window made and new roof and raised a couple of feet, would vote as I liked all his life. Has no vote this time because his landladies pay the taxes.

The following extracts refer to the second election, in 1835.

7 May 1835 I met Sowden. I asked him for his vote. No! he would not vote at all. I said I was sorry for it. He said he had friends on both sides and none but independent men should vote. Then, said I, there would not be as many hundred of voters as there are thousands. Better, said I, to take one side — those who took neither made no friends and in case of anything happening had nobody to take to. It was as if they set themselves on a hill to be pelted by all parties. S(owden) said *that in some counties the tenants talked of turning off the landlords* instead of the landlords turning off the tenants. Well, said I, then we must make as good a fight as we can — perhaps you may get the better — we must try for it, but is not this like the unions and men taking against the masters? S(owden) asked if I should not want a good deal of rough stuff for my job at Mytholm (meaning coal water wheel). Yes! said I, but I must think of my friends for this, and then wished S — good day. W.K. — told me, S — was an arrant yellow ...

2 September 1835 Had Mr Sowden. Sorry he had offended — hoped I should look over it — would have given me his vote but had been first canvassed by the yellows and had promised not to vote at all. Otherwise did not care 6d. how he voted. Then, said I, will you vote with me? Yes. Very well, said I, then I will think no more of what has passed — meaning he might keep his farm. Said I would not take a new tenant who would not give me his vote but I had not meant to send away an old one. However, I must now consider S — as a new tenant and ask his vote. He promised to give it me. I said dinner was waiting, ordered him beer, and came away.

However, in spite of the fact that Miss Lister thus controlled about fifty votes, her candidate came out at the bottom of the poll. In a letter to Lady Vere Cameron (31 December 1832) she wrote:- So thoroughly unexpected was my disappointment at the loss of Mr James Wortley's election, I have never got up my political spirits since. All the *soi-disant* knowing ones, and *soi-disant* leading people, had made themselves so sure of success, that the failure burst upon us like a thunderbolt. There was decidedly clever management on the other side, and this and the popular cry bore down everything. I hardly thought myself capable of such strong political excitement and mortification. I fear the elections are bad enough — far too many anti-church men. I am completely sick of public events. The unions are still in full force. Many of the Delvers (stone quarriers) have turned in to their work again; but they have gained the day, and the advance of wages.

Paris. Rue neuve Luxembourg, No 4. Thursday 1 August 1833.

After all my pains-taking, my dear aunt, on Sunday, it was impossible, even at eleven fifteen a.m. to get thro' troops and people to the post-office; but I hope my letter did get off on Monday. Do tell me always on what days you receive them. There was no stirring during the three days of fête, no getting anything done before, and no doing anything even for one's self till Tuesday. I then went to Lafitte's, and got your letter, and Washington's, which last (for economy's sake) I shall probably answer on part of this sheet, and ask you to put it under cover, and send it as you like, or best can. You seem to be all going on quite well at Shibden; and this is, of course, the greatest comfort I can have in my absence. I am delighted at your having hired a niece of Cordingley's brother-in-law ... Her age is very proper — her having been so long with an invalid is everything. Never mind being a little countryfied in appearance, and manners. One may learn at thirty; and you will see she will improve with a little of your teaching. You have done very right and very well. Do give my kind remembrances to Cordingley, and tell her I cannot help thinking, as I am sure she must think too, that the death of her mother must be rather a mercy, than a severe infliction of providence. Tell John I have heard again from Mrs Lawton who has heard Martha read, given her her catechism to learn more perfectly and is much pleased with her wish to improve herself. He may set himself quite at ease about Martha. His son's schooling is not much; and *I* mean to pay it — perhaps, my dear aunt, you will be so good as order about this for me, saying, that I think, as this boy is paid for, John, seeing the necessity of educating his children as well as he can, ought to pay what he now thinks he is to pay for the boy, for the little girl. If she is made a pretty good scholar, she, too, may be helped by and by, in some way or other; but, if she cannot both read and write well, I know nothing that can be done for her. John is well enough off to give up the little they gain by card-setting, to enable them to do better for themselves and for him too hereafter ... It is broiling hot; but I cannot move yet. I have yet a great deal to do of one sort or other. The King was not shot at on Sunday; and all went off quietly; and, on the whole, he had reason to be satisfied with his reception. I did not go to the window I told you of, with Mrs & Miss Barlow — the crowd was so dense, I thought myself best at home; and, besides, did not like being cooped up eight or nine hours without being able to stir — for once in the place, there you must stay. You see I mean to take special care of myself. I came here from the Hotel de la Terrace, on Monday, where I live in twice the comfort for half the money. Eugénie's mother has come to see her, a very nice person, and she has put us into the way of managing beautifully. Both Eugénie and Ths seem so anxious to do all they can, I really think we shall get on very well. I shall calculate by and by; but Eugénie's mother included I don't spend for living so much as half what I did. Eugénie markets, and in the nicest cleanest way you ever saw, prepares our soup, and bouilli, and cutlets, and rice pudding, so that I have only perhaps one thing of some sort to get from the restaurateur. Thomas washes up, and does the rooms; and the ten days longer I shall be here, will get on beautifully. If we can possibly keep up to going on as well as we do now, I shall think my servants treasures. Thomas gets on very well with the carriage — he repeats after me all I tell him, and I have not had a *laquais de place*, except for the first errand to the Embassy. I left my card for Lord Granville on Tuesday. Cte de Noé and Louise gone to their chateau in the south — the countess and her second daughter delighted to see me. Poor Mme Cuvier received me quite like an old friend, and told me all about the suddenness of Cuvier's death, not exactly cholera, but a rapid paralysis of all the vital organs occasioned by the state of the atmosphere during that dreadful epidemic. Poor Langier, the chemical professor, died of the cholera. My other Jardin des Plantes friends are in the country; but I shall probably see them all before I go.

14

A HASTY RETURN FROM COPENHAGEN

1833

In August 1833 Anne, accompanied by her Danish friend, Sophie Ferrall, travelled via the Netherlands and Germany to Copenhagen where Anne was introduced to all the people of importance who invited her to a round of balls and parties.

This trip was intended as the first stage of her long cherished dream of visiting Russia but alas! after three months of happy socializing, she heard that her aunt Anne was seriously ill. She immediately set off for home, escorted by Lord Hillsborough.

> Rendsburg — at the post-house door.
> Tuesday one thirty p.m. 3 December 1833.

Dear Countess de Blucher,

My date will tell you something — that it is half past one before our getting even so far on our way. If we can get to Hamburg in time, it will be all we can possibly do. I leave you to guess my feverish state of anxiety. Lord Hillsborough[1] and I get on beautifully, he is really very good, and considerate. He has just promised me in his letter to Mr Browne to send my message of kindest regards &c. to you, and explain why I could not possibly write — but it occurs to me to write a little in the carriage, and if, when we are off again, I can manage to go on in spite of the jolting, you shall have this pencil scrawl. We reached Korsoer at six thirty on Sunday morning, and breakfasted and waited there till eleven. The steamer is not allowed to take carriages over on a Sunday. Luckily the wind was fair, we sent off the carriage by a sailing vessel at nine, and it arrived as soon as we. We were three hours and twenty minutes on the *rough* water, and almost everybody but Lord H — and Count D'Ahrenfeldt[2] (I cannot answer for spelling — I mean the rich Count I saw one morning *chez vous*) was sick. As usual, I did not know my friend again, in spite of all his kindness and attention, till he introduced himself to Lord H -, and asked us to dine with him at the Inn at Nyborg, which we very gladly did, and found both himself and his friend, Countess Plessen's brother, most gentlemanly and agreeable. Lord H — and I did not want this attention more to make us charmed with Copenhagen and all the kind people we saw there. We intend to sing your praises far and near, and to prove whatever be the faults of the English, they are not ungrateful. Off from Nyborg at a quarter before five, and, to the credit of prince Christian's government of Fynen, reached Odense (four miles) in two hours and twenty-five minutes. Oh! that the roads were everywhere as good. Oh! that the King in his most gracious pleasure would make him (prince Christian) Govenor of Schleswig! It was near one in the morning of yesterday when we reached Middelfart — the moon hid her light, the rain fell in torrents and the wind blew a stiff gale; both my people outside were wet thro', so I would make them stop to get their clothes dried. We were off again at six am, passed the little Belt in ten minutes, and regretted that we had not *seen* more of Fynen. No horses — my Lord's dispatches cleared away the difficulty — (I could not have got on without him) — the post-master took the four horses from a waggon standing by, and off we were. It was half past one this morning when we reached Flensburg — the roads were bad enough before — here they began to be terrible — and we waded thro' turf and sand and water to Schleswig and thence to Rendsburg and are now waving across to Braunstedt, six and a half miles, as well as we can. I am holding my writing-case on my arm, and writing as well as I can — but it is not in vain; for Lord H — says 'You know Miss Ferrall told you she could read your *short* writing' so heaven grant she can read my long! I wish you saw us. At six thirty this morning, two hours from Schleswig, after a tremendous jolt, down came the rumble on Thomas's side. Luckily, nobody was the worse, and after tying it up with ropes, on we went, my Lord astride of the luggage on the boot with his face towards the carriage and Thomas on the off wheeler, and thus we entered Schleswig! No time for smiths and repairs, so we merely tied on the travelling bag behind, mounted Thomas on horseback to ride after us, and Lord H -, having a tolerable seat on the boot, we were going on pretty decently. He lost his hat in the storm before reaching Middelfart, so that the *Southwester* is the only resource. After your abuse of my travelling cap, I did not put it on the first night; but I soon found that beauty can make no long stand against utility. We eat as we can — generally in the carriage — sometimes we find cold meat — sometimes only cheese and bread. It was lucky I brought away my six bottles of wine. I suspected we might be glad enough of it *en route*. I wish we could have *seen* more of the country. Schleswig is beautifully situated; and I am much taken with Rendsburg — the fortifications are singularly pretty — the canal and shipping between the lines of circumvallation are very striking. The post-master cheered me with the assurance that we should reach Hamburg in time. We shall drive up to the steamer, and go on board immediately. I suppose we are to be under weigh at three in the morning tomorrow. We have a chance of a fair wind, and a rough passage of course at this season. I get more and more anxious — perhaps I shall not stay in London even to have the rumble mended. Do give my kind regards to the De Hagemanns — my love to Lady Harriet, and tell her I will write a few lines from London *if I possibly can*, but if not, she shall hear from me immediately on my arrival at home. Now that I have written so much, I shall send it you, tho' it is really a shame. Lord H — and I agree in thinking princess Christian the finest woman we have anywhere seen of long — he says prince Frederick is not half so bad as he is said to be. In short, do be assured, the attentions we have received are not thrown away — tell your sister to think a little better of the English — we are almost always better than we seem? If you have any opportunity do be so good as give my compliments to Count Vargas de Bidimar, and tell him how very much I am obliged for all his so kind attention. I shall be delighted to hear from you. Don't pother yourself, but don't send your paper half full, because your sister has promised me better things. (The letter ends here and was apparently never sent.)

Hamburg. Thursday evening 5 December 1833.

My dear aunt,

I write this here, to be ready for the first post. Your so indifferent account of yourself, and your talking of your leg *taking bad ways*, determined me to be set off as soon as I could, and here I am. I did not wait to write from Copenhagen. In fact, I received your letter several hours later than I ought to have done, and was therefore too late for the next post, and was off at the same time as the post following. The roads are terrible; but we have got on very tolerably, and are all quite well. We had no vexatious delays on the road, as I brought Lord Hillsborough with me, who had dispatches; and, consequently, the post-master was obliged to give us horses, and send us on, as fast as possible — by this means, too, I avoided all custom-house annoyances, and have really had a very good journey. I almost count upon being with you nearly as soon as my letter. Do pray tell Cordingley to have my room ready, and a bed for Thomas. I think he had better sleep in the parlour-chamber above you. I shall provide for Eugénie. You would be quite astonished to know how well I have managed, and with how little inconvenience I shall be back again at Shibden. I only hope, and trust, I shall find you better than, from your letter, I dare expect. I am sure you will be glad to see me. All I entreat of you, is not to be nervous about me. I am perfectly well, and only anxious to see you. You might be quite sure I should come. Tell Marian that I shall not be long after my letter. My best love to you all. Ever my dear aunt, very affectionately yours, A.L. -

Anne's hurried journey was rewarded by finding her aunt recovered.

---

[1] Arthur Blundell Sandys Trumbull (Hill), Marques of Devonshire, and Earl of Hillsborough, 1788-1845.

[2] Count von Ahlefeldt.

15

SWITZERLAND REVISITED

1834

Letter begun by Anne Lister, and continued by Ann Walker, to Anne Lister senior, at Shibden Hall.

Geneva. Tuesday evening. 22 July 1834.

It was only this afternoon, my dear aunt, we returned here, after a most agreeable and healthy excursion among the mountains. We left here, as my last letter would tell you, on the 3rd inst., and have enjoyed our absence exceedingly. The only drawback was the impossibility of receiving or sending letters; and we began to be very impatient for home news ... I am very glad you will not want us back again before the end of next month, and that this delay will not inconvenience Marian. I only hope we shall lose none of our good looks before you see us. These seventeen days upon muleback, making what is called the grand tour of Mont Blanc, have quite cured us both. We have really done great things — people would hardly believe us if we told them. Adny's strength improved daily; and you can't think what a nice little traveller she is — always pleased — always *right*. We made Chamouni our headquarters, and were quite sorry to leave them. We mounted George on the Baggage mule, and left Eugénie with the carriage at Sallenche, about twenty miles from Chamouni, large carriages not being able to get nearer. George did very well; and we enjoyed our mountain wanderings exceedingly. We traversed all the principal passes immediately round Mont Blanc, over snow, and ice, and rocks, and precipices. Such scrambling as nobody ever saw for four-footed animals in England. George will (have) fine tales to tell. We heard Eugénie and him laughing at a fine rate this morning behind the carriage. Of course, our hotels were not always magnificent. We spent one night at the hospice of the Great St Bernard, and crossed the little St Bernard also (the route which the majority of authors agree to have been that of Hannibal) and, in fact, we did nearly twice as much as travellers usually do. We were twice at Cormayeur, came up with two of the King's sons at Aosta, spent a day at Bex, and two nights at Martigny. At Bex we had a tremendous storm of thunder and lightning and rain, and, in returning to Martigny, had a striking example of the uncertainty of roads carried over mountain torrents — the stream that had seemed a mere brook in the morning, had swept away the bridge, filled its bed and a great breadth on either side with mud, and pieces of rock, and torn up trees, so that two or three hours after all was over we were carried thro' on men's backs, and our little char dragged by men who drove our frightened mule before by main force. Martigny is always infested by mosquitoes, and we have not recovered their bites. But I must not run on at this rate, till I have answered the business part of your letter. I am very glad of your account of George Robinson. I quite agree with Mr Parker in believing him a very honest man — but if a man has nothing, what can he do. I trust, however, trade really is better, and that George will weather the storm. He *has* the mill on lease. I explained to Mr Parker all I meant; and I am sure by his delivering the notice himself, that he will do it right — he will make it understood that nobody else knows of it, and that it is merely provisional ... A.L. -

(Letter continued by Ann Walker)

My dear aunt,

Anne has told you our route over the mountains, but I find she has not given you any description of the magnificent hotels we met with. At Mottets we slept between the cows and the hay loft, and at the village des Ferret there were two rooms, for us, guides, George, and the poor widow with eight children. We thought at first George must sleep at the foot of our bed, but a bed was at last contrived for him in the room with the family and the guides. In our little apartment, which was so low, that we could touch the ceiling with our hands when we were in bed, we had two sickly children that cried a great part of the night. The people were very civil and attentive, and we were really very tolerably comfortable, and I assure you these little adventures not only served us to laugh at, at the time, but they made us feel the comfort and value afterwards, of a good hotel. I am sure you would have been very much amused if you could have seen us in our mountain scrambles, trudging sometimes almost up to our knees in snow; on passing one of the declivities George, who was shewing off his agility in getting over the snow, unfortunately slipped, and down he went for a considerable distance, and must have gone to the bottom, but for a piece of rock against which he contrived to stop himself. There was no danger, and he was not in the least hurt, perhaps it made him a little more careful afterwards. I asked George one day how he liked the mountains, and if he had ever seen any so high before; he told me yes, he thought the mountain we were then upon (the Brevent), a very fine one, was very like one of the Hambledon Hills called the White Mare. I think I may quite assure you, that you have no occasion to feel anxious now about Anne's health, I think I may say she is quite well, certainly better than I have known her in England. As for myself, I expect to surprise everybody on my return ... Ann Walker.

Hotel de l'Europe, Lyons, Sunday night 10 August 1834.

My dear aunt, we do indeed think, and talk of you, and you all very much. I hope good tidings will welcome our return to Paris. It will probably be the 19th or 20th before we get there; but you shall hear from us, on our arrival. Tomorrow we sleep at St Etienne, the Newcastle of France (I mean for coal), and hope to reach Clermont, in Auvergne, on Tuesday. We shall spend two or three days there, and then make the best of our way to Meurice's, where, for this time, it is probable we shall try to be taken in. The weather is so *very* hot, great exertion is not easy, or we should travel more rapidly; but we hope to be at home about the time mentioned in my last. A(nn) has not flattered Grenoble in her account of it. Had I painted the picture, it would have been coloured more agreeably. I was in no degree

184

disappointed with this fine part of Dauphiny, where there is land let at the rate of ten to twelve pounds a Daywork — three crops in a year, and hemp above eleven feet high! Ground is so valuable, the Isère and the Drac are kept amazingly well within bounds and the standing waters A — mentions are reservoirs into which the river water is turned when very muddy, and left to deposit a sediment afterwards used as manure. Voiron is a thriving little town famous for its linen cloth. You see even in all the villages around a wheel at every door, and since the disturbances here.[1] one or two of the great merchants have built (set up) large cotton-printing, and silk manufactories — but Lyons is now, and is likely to be, quiet; and trade is recovering itself. A(dny) should have told you our King's velvet[2] (nearly two yards wide) is to be 250 francs or £10 a yard, before it is embroidered with gold. We read prayers this morning, and went out about one, not returning to dinner till after seven. There are several Roman remains that few people see, tho' they are better worth seeing than many that everybody runs after ... I hope M(ariana) has got my letter from Geneva, and that she is better. I ... begged that I might find a letter from her in Paris. We really must rest there two or three days, or the heat will have melted so much of us away, that you will not think us looking sufficiently *rotund*. I hope the business about the carriage will have had time enough to be settled while I am in Paris. They made me pay duty at Calais; and I appealed against this to the director general of the customs, but I shall not delay beyond my own time on this account ... We shall return by Calais — once in London, we shall be very impatient to finish our journey. I will write, if but a few lines, both from there and Paris, but, with one thing or other, I am really very busy ... The mountain air certainly did us a great deal of good — this is a beautiful city, but neither A — nor I would like to live here. We are not fond of being too near rivers, or too much in the bottoms of valleys. Shibden is neither too high nor too low, and we shall return with pleasure ... A.L. -

---

[1] In 1834 Lyons was the scene of violent industrial and political disturbances.

[2] Manufactured at Lyons for the King's drawing room at Windsor.

Letter from Miss Ann Walker, to Miss Anne Lister senior, at Shibden Hall.

Clermont, 16 August 1834.

My dear aunt,

We were so late in leaving Lyons on Monday that we slept at Rive-de-Gier instead of St Etienne, both places are as black and dirty as Low Moor, and I am sure you would have been much amused could you have seen what wretched looking beings we were; so besmeared with black dust, that it was impossible to know the real colour of our skin. The coal pits are much larger than any we have in Yorkshire; we went down one or rather I should say Anne, for I descended only part of the way, and returned as I found it cold, and was a little afraid of the damp air; Anne, however, was very much pleased with the pit, and the next day, she went to another which is on the surface of the earth, and the coal got from it, as we hew stone from our stone quarries. The country thereabouts reminded us very much of Shibden. We left St Etienne on Wednesday, slept at Montbrison, and set out early the next morning in the hope of reaching Clermont that night, but as we were unfortunately detained at La Bergère an hour and twenty minutes for horses, besides having been previously detained on the road, to change with another carriage, which is really a great bother, we stopped at Pont-du-Chateau, the last stage before Clermont; our accommodation there was not of the best, and moreover they told us that perhaps a *vetturino* might come in, during the night, to repose on one of the five beds in our apartment. There was not a lock or fastener of any kind on the door, but Anne, whose resources never fail, barred it most effectively with the handle of our little boiling apparatus for tea, however, we had so much *company* in our beds we were quite glad to get up at four in the morning and come here to breakfast. We congratulated ourselves upon the very comfortable apartment we had engaged, when soon after breakfast, we thought we should melt away. Eugénie then told us that the kitchen was exactly underneath, Anne immediately spoke to Madame of the Hotel, who changed it, for a much more airy room, tho' not quite so large, however this is of little consequence, as it is greatly for our comfort, the change was a great favour, as it is the animal fair at Clermont, and every place is full. Anne is gone to the Puy de Dome, a very celebrated mountain elevated 4,800 feet above the level of the sea; there is said to be a magnificent view from its summit, to obtain it one must start from here at four o'clock in the morning, as the only method of ascending the steepest and highest part of the mountain is on foot. I thought it much the best to stay quietly at the Inn. Anne gave George his choice whether he would go, or stay, and I am very glad to say he chose the former, and they set out about four, in a nice little carriage, which would convey them about two leagues on the road to Aurillac, and thence they would have to walk. I do hope Anne will be rewarded by a sight of the fine view, but the morning was so brilliant and hot here at eight, I *fear* she may be disappointed. I laughed and told her as she chose to run away, I should write to you, and fill all the paper, not leaving her a morsel, however my heart relents so much, I have concluded to leave one end for her. We talk of going to Vichy tomorrow, about thirty miles, which we hope will enable us to reach Paris on the 20th, or in good time on 21st ... We talk much of our return to Shibden how pretty it will look, and how busy we shall be. Once off from Paris we shall travel as fast as our horses can take us but with French horses and tackle, the fastest appears but slow to English people ... A.W.

Paris 21 August 1834.

My dear aunt, we are this moment arrived, safe and well, from the baths of Vichy, twenty or thirty miles from Clermont. I went to the top of the Puy de Dome, and to the bottom of the silver mines, and was amply rewarded for my hard day's work. But I can think of none of these things just now — they have sent all my letters to Geneva; and I am quite in despair, but I hope there is no commission, at least from you, that you will be disappointed at my not doing. The letters would be back here next week; but I shall not wait for them, as I am sure you would rather have us at home. I trust all is going on well. I am in a great hurry just now, for fear of being too late even for the great post. It is *very* hot here, as well as farther south. You shall have a few lines on our arrival in London ... A.L. -

London. 26 Dover Street. Wednesday evening 27 August 1834.

My dear aunt,

We are this moment arrived from Rochester where we took a long sleep after crossing the water ... We have several little things to do here, but hope to get off tomorrow evening, via Richmond, to take coffee with Lady S(tuart), this will not be *very much* round, and not delay us more than a few hours, that it is possible we may reach Shibden late on Saturday. Except the bed, a kettle of boiling water will be enough to have prepared for us; and let John, and John only, sit up till twelve, but no later. We will make an effort to avoid travelling on Sunday morning, but we return by Lawton, that, if Mrs Lawton be at home, seeing her will take an hour or two ... We reached the Ship Inn at Dover at forty minutes past nine yesterday morning, after an excellent passage of two hours forty minutes, neither of us, none of us sick. We should have been here sooner, but could not get the carriage *landed* till after one ... A.L. -

16

THE LAST JOURNEY

Through Six Countries To Russia 1839-1840

Shibden affairs occupied Anne between 1835 and 1838 — her coal mines, building a Norman tower on the west gable of the house for her books, letting Northgate House which she had converted into a hotel, and local elections. After the deaths of her father and her aunt in 1836, she made a short tour with her friend Ann Walker, to Belgium, France and the Pyrenees. At Liège Anne 'went to the bottom of one of the deepest coalpits said to be 400 yards deep, so it might be. The descent by ladders was no joke; the ascent in the panier (great wooden box that will bring up two tons of coal at once) took six minutes, the steam engine that pulled us having forty horse power.'

They spent three weeks on mule back and mountaineering in the Pyrenees and after climbing one of the highest mountains, Anne sent the following message to *Galignani's Messenger*: 'Miss Lister will be much obliged to Messrs. Galignani to insert the following paragraph in the next edition of their *Messenger* after receiving this note:- We noticed some days ago, the ascent of the Prince de la Moscowa and his brother, Mr Edgar Ney, with five guides, to the summit of the Vignemale, hitherto thought inaccessible. We find that an English lady had, four days before, ascended with three guides to the same summit, which, thought inaccessible from the French side, is not more difficult of ascent, from the Spanish side, towards the east, than mountains in general.'

St Sauveur. Monday evening 26 August 1838.

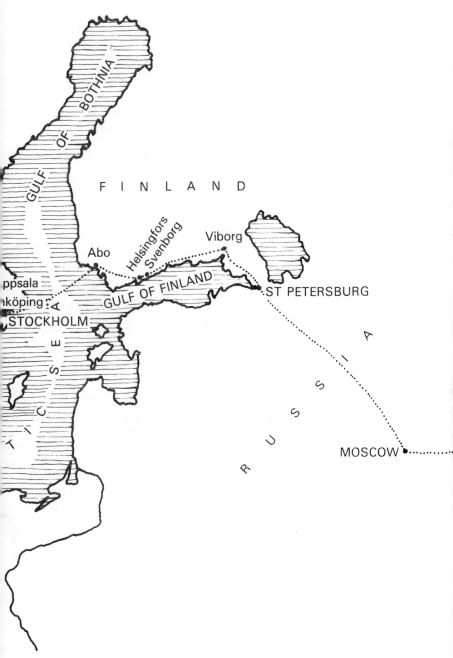

Anne Lister's route through six countries to Russia 1839-40

In April 1839 Miss Lister's thoughts again turned towards travel. This journey to Russia, via Belgium, Holland, Germany, Denmark, Sweden and Finland was to be the longest she had ever undertaken, and it was to prove her last. She and Ann Walker reached St Petersburgh on September 17 1839.

The letters relating to the stay in Moscow are chiefly brief notes of invitation from Russian friends. The two travellers had not intended staying so long in Moscow, but they were obliged to wait until the bad weather was over, and the roads suitable for sledges. Princess Olga Dolgarouky's father offered to lend his courier, for which Miss Lister was very grateful. Before leaving Moscow (on February 5 1840) Anne wrote to a few of her friends to relate her adventures up to date, and to inform them of the projected six months' trip to the Caucasus.

Moscow. Monday 13 January 1840.

To me, my dearest Vere, it seems age upon age since I wrote to you nor, thinking of you perpetually as I do, can I in any way satisfactorily account for so long an epistolary silence. I hope *you* have thought it long, for I could not bear you to give up thinking of me, tho' I do appear to have taken so little pains to prevent it. No! No! you must think of me still with all the affection you can spare. Being so long without hearing from you, is at last an absolute discomfort that rouses me to my writing desk ... By the way, did you not receive an *edible* proof of my thinking of you at Christiania? I sent off four barrels of anchovies, all which, I hope, reached their respective destinations. You would hear of me up to that time, and of our *hydrophobia*, and going by Calais. We had *our* rooms (yours and mine) at Ghent, the same house at Antwerp, and in the cathedral gazed on the same Rubens. I thought of you very much. You are oftener in my mind than you imagine. Copenhagen had, as usual in summer, *disgorged* herself into the country. To see Lady Harriet caused us an interesting little détour. She was looking not a day older than seven years ago, tho' perhaps rather thinner and rather nervous at seeing me so unexpectedly. Alba is a nice girl, and Frederic will be all the better for a voyage per steam to *chez vous* and *chez moi*. You know we crossed the Sound (how lovely!) to Helsinborg, and bought a little open carriage at Götheborg for our Norway (tour?), and were delighted with the falls (the series of rapids) at Trölhattan. My last letters left us in admiration of the beauties of Christiania, and setting off in high spirits for a regular Norwegian tour beginning with the excursion to Gaousta-fell. Nothing can exceed in picturesque beauty and scenery from Christiania to Bolkesoë. I almost venture to say, all you have read and heard is not exaggerated. Have you read Bremner's new work? Of course, he is in raptures with country, men, and things . . . His Russia[1] is, I believe, défendu in Russia — no great wonder — I just looked into him in London. You shall have my critique, *viva voce*, one of these days. But to return to Bolkesoë — we just arrived in time to see it in its beauty, and no more. Our bright prospect changed — rain and mist surrounded us; and, after waiting two wet days, and being well advised that we had no chance of fair weather on this side the mountains, we reluctantly turned back, *steamed* it from Christiania to Götheborg, found sunshine again on the Swedish side, and, resuming our English carriage, posted on to Stockholm very agreeably. Good roads, no *désagrémens*. Carbonnades and game in the towns, and good bread, butter, milk, eggs and *pancakes* everywhere. Small pull-out sofa-beds, but clean sheets and pleasant dreams. We had a Götheborg Scotch-naturalized-Swede coachman (Götheborg is half Scotch), and settled ourselves, without any trouble, at Stockholm, in a large, handsome, comfortable apartment at the hotel Garni, our little civil landlord, Mr Confectioner Behrings, one of the most accommodating and best of men and Swedes, his parting present of warm comforts (comfits) lasted us to here, as did also our loaf of Deventer gingerbread, the best of all gingerbread kind. Lord Durham went from Götheborg to Stockholm by the Göthe-canal, a cheap, excellent plan; but we had seen Trölhattan at our leisure, and preferred *coasting* the lakes to *steaming* them. Wenner is too large, the shores too distant, and too tame. Wetter less, but too much in the same style. Malar very beautiful, but lovelier still the scattered cottage, and the sunbeam's play along the little rock-girt, pine shaded lakelets of northern Sweden. Lady Harriet did not over-praise the beauties of Stockholm — the view from the mountain, well enough called the mountain of Moses, is quite charming. Our fortnight's tour, via Upsala (the pink mead at old Upsala as good as the best pink champagne) to *all* the mines, from *top to bottom*, was very interesting, and we had a beautiful little extra bit of Dalecarlia where, of course, we grew enamoured of Gustaf Vasa. Of Charles John, and the National-School-mania of Oscar, other people will tell you better than I. We liked the good, honest Swedes, who were always civil, and always ready *to do our liking*. We had no disappointment but that which Heaven showered down in Norway, interesting land of fell and fjord that we should like to see more of. Its language delighted us — better far than all your German for English etymologies. I shall write to Lady Harriet *sometime*. Do tell her with my love, and kind regards to Mr de H(agemann) who was really all kindness and attention, that I hardly forgive them for not making me study Danish, that is, my pet Norsk, and Norges Aloste historie, at Copenhagen. But how my paper wastes, I have not left Stockholm! We bade her goodnight at ten on Friday September 6 in a good Åbo steamer, the most agreeable of her kind. Beautiful voyage in point of weather and of island scenery scattered over the dark blue *wave*. No! Surface of the gulph, for all was smooth as glass. We cast anchor the following night, wanting light to wind our way amid the island-group; but we soon ran the twelve or fourteen miles, and landed at Åbo at six thirty a.m. on the Sunday. But never mind 'dates and distances', and interstices. Helsingfors is charming, the young, and beautiful, and present capital of Finland. Tell your friends to go to the Society's house, and look over the lovely bay, its islands, its Sveaborg, its dark blue waters studded with shipping. One eighty-four close under the town, and four more, and two or three forty-four frigates, sloops and brigs in the offing, besides merchant and small craft. It was a lovely sunset, morning, noonday scene. Laygard was too much in break-neck haste, but buy him, nevertheless. Abate dangers and *désagrémens* (we travelled by daylight in fine weather and had a Swedish coachman), and he is a good guide. He is the H.L. of the Handbook for Northern Europe, published by Murray last summer, price 10/-. We took our time, and enjoyed ourselves, and slept and fared *à merveille*. It was a beautiful afternoon (Tuesday September 17) as we drove over the magnificent Neva into the city of palaces. If *you* have (*I* have not) had time and patience to read thro' the ponderous Granville,[2] you know St Petersburgh as well as it is possible to know it by description. They say all he wrote is true; and so it ought, considering that he did not give himself time to forget, but, as they say, went about in society, at parties, with his tablets in his hand, and, to the joy or terror of his friends, did indeed catch and note the breath and *manners living as they rose*. Do not be the least afraid for the column of Alexander, there is a little bit of longitudinal crack, but is is of no consequence. The exterior of the magnificent Isaac church is to be finished next summer. The iron-work of the dome (by a Scotsman, Beard) is well worth the examination of any professional man, and you would be repaid the trouble of mounting by the panoramic view of this extraordinary city. Extraordinary creation of that extraordinary man Peter Veliki. I have only got a few words of Russian, but it is impossible not to learn and remember *Veliki*, great. The winter palace was under repair, and therefore we did not, could not see it, but the matchless Hermitage took us three days. There *is* a catalogue of the pictures, and one of the best of all the innumerable catalogues I have ever seen. The Keepsake for this year reached us a week or two ago. Lord Londonderry was unlucky to find the Hermitage staircase so dirty, and still more so to note 'a great gallery painted, communicates with the salons' as if quite unconscious of the interest and value of this beautiful copy of the Loggia of Raphael. You, who have spent so many hours at the Vatican, would know how to appreciate the magnificence of Catherine in ordering this copy. In fact, this gallery is now shewn to everyone. But Lady L — had no eye for Raffaello — she makes no note of the Vierge d'Albe! She mentions Paul Potter's[3] rough dog, worthy all she says of it, but did she not see the group of cows? Never mind the name, (*Vache qui pisse*). Is there not a waterfall of the name that everybody goes to see; and may not she whose eye has gazed on the beauties of a Venus or an Apollo, look at this poor cow? I remember the *bull* at Amsterdam, and prefer the *cow*. There are four charming Claudes in the same *salle (de vache)* morning, evening, noon, and night. But no more — there are many *chefs d'oeuvre we ought* to have had, and many *we might* have had; but since *we*, in our *artless* folly, let them go, I am not sorry to have seen them where they are. The riches in the precious metals and precious stones are extraordinarily great; but they are also great here (Moscow) and great in all the celebrated churches and convents. But St P(etersburgh) is the favoured capital of an enormous empire whose head *has a head*, and who has gathered into this magnificent *berceau* of his family more that is worth seeing than most people have time to see, or even to find out. The Ecole des Mines, the Museum of the Academy, the Imperial Library &c., &c., &c., are very remarkable. Well might Napoleon long to tear away the French archives sequestered during the madness of the first revolution, but they were packed up, and would have been at Archangel before he could have passed the Valdai hills. The Russians are an *interesting* (people?), the link between Europe and Asia, between the nomads and the settled. But they should be studied carefully and at leisure, and not written about from notes in a diligence or a *kibitka* by those who neither understand their customs, their circumstances, nor their tongue. Napoleon sacked and desecrated their churches, and, after that, could never find an honest friend in Russia. The Greek catholic worship is a step above the Roman catholic in splendour and antiquity. I have got accustomed to the Byzantine style of church, and gilded domes, and silver, and sky-blue, and sea green, and every colour you can name. The beauty of Moscow is indescribable; and the Kremlin unrivalled. Dr Johnson makes some such observation as, the good of travelling is in enlarging our number of analyses. I hope to be richer in these by and by; and then it will be more flattering to this fair city to repeat, that I still think it the most beautiful town I have ever seen. I wish Lady Emmeline Wortley would come here. She would write better than Lady L -. Lord Royston's few letters are the best *multum-in-parvo* I have read. We are waiting for snow to go over some part of his route. We arrived here in five days (good road and weather) on October 12, too late to see all here, and reach Odessa (comfortably) for the winter, as we once intended. I shall send you this letter by the post direct from here, not caring to risk its loss by troubling my banker at St (Petersburgh) to send it to the Embassy. I shall

---

[1] Eobert Bremner — Excursions in the interior of Russia, including sketches of the character and policy of the Emperor Nicolas, scenes in St Petersburg, etc. 1839.

[2] Augustus B. Granville — St Petersburg. A journal of travels to and from the capital, through Flanders, the Rhenish provinces, Prussia, Russia, Poland, Silesia, Saxony, the Federated States of Germany and France. 2 Vols., London, 1828.

[3] Paul Potter (1625-1654), Dutch animal painter.

write to you again from *somewhere* before my return. We hope to be off in a few days, by the first trainage for Nijnii, Kazan, Seratov, Astrakhan, &c., &c., to Odessa. I wish *very much* to know whether this letter weighs more than half an ounce and what you pay for it. We have English papers now and then. Talk of me to my little Sibbella. Ever very affectionately yours, A.L. -

You had best direct to the care of Messrs. R. & H. Hunt, Hamburg. Handbook should have been here in winter — handsome houses, balls in the best Parisian style, and a great many pretty girls. One *dame* in particular, is one of the finest women I ever saw, and a Venus de Moscova.

Moscow. Monday 3 February 1840.

I have not heard from you, dearest Lady Stuart, since leaving London! I know how troublesome it is to you to write, but I always feel anxious to hear how you are, and I have begged Vere to tell me how you have passed the winter. It has been unusually severe here; they say the seasons here are much changed for the worse of late. There was hardly any rain in the summer; and the heat was so great, and the earth so parched, that the harvest was ruined, the cattle died of want, the forests took fire, and some hundreds of acres were consumed; and, in short in spite of all the efforts of the noblesse, the peasantry is suffering severely. It is a bad year for travelling in Russia, but we must hope for a fine spring. We shall be off before day-light on Wednesday morning for Nijenii Novogorod, Kazan, and the Volga to Astrakhan and the Caucasus. The cold was so great, we gave up all idea of Siberia and the Urals for the present. After having *parcouru* the Alps and Pyrenees, the Caucasus will be doubly interesting. But I dare not hope that we shall be able to make many excursions beyond the range of the Russian troops, as we have no fancy for being taken prisoners. Our three armed men (a Government courier, our own Russian courier, and Gross) could not do much against the swords and rifles of the Circassians. We travel in two *kibitkas* — the one arranged for ourselves is admirably convenient. Our greatest anxiety now is to reach Astrakhan before the breaking up of the river, but if we cannot manage this, we shall put our vehicles on wheels, and amuse ourselves, no doubt, exceedingly well, till we can pursue our journey to Tiflis, which we proposed making headquarters for as long as may be necessary for seeing all we can. From Tiflis it is our present plan to go by the fine new road to the Crimea, and thence to Odessa where it *may be* July before we arrive ... We are delighted at the thought of our journey, and much taken with the idea of driving 400 versts on the Volga ... I hope this and my note to Lady Stuart de Rothesay, under cover to Lord Stuart, will go from St Petersburgh by the Embassy bag. We saw by the English papers that his lordship had been on a mission to H.M. of Hanover. The Hagemanns will be very sorry for the death of the King of Denmark ... A. Lister.

17

THE LAND OF TONGUES AND MOUNTAINS. (THE CAUCASUS)

1840

Draft letter to Mrs Mariana Lawton, Lawton, Cheshire.

Tiflis. Monday 4 May 1840.

In my letter from Moscow, my dearest Mary, I merely told you of our going southwards; it was then not quite decided, on account of roads and one thing or other, that we should take exactly our present route. Nothing, however, could have answered better; and we are delighted with our journey. You will trace us on the map, and see that we have made a tolerably long, and very interesting detour ... We are already in our fourth week here, as if we were at home, so settled and acquainted. The society is most agreeable, the weather delightful, the town and country *interesting* beyond description. In fact, our journey has been a climax of interest, increasing at every step. The site of Nijni is magnificent — its buildings for the great fair are a palace-bazaar where, during this one month per annum (August) above nine millions sterling are turned over! We were impatient to see Kazan; and this fine old Tatar capital did not disappoint us — it is full of interest past and present. We had a Tatar breakfast, and were admitted into a Tatar haram, and attended divine worship in the great mosque. We have all read of these things; but it is nothing — the descriptions are good; but they cannot give the impress of reality. You would see in

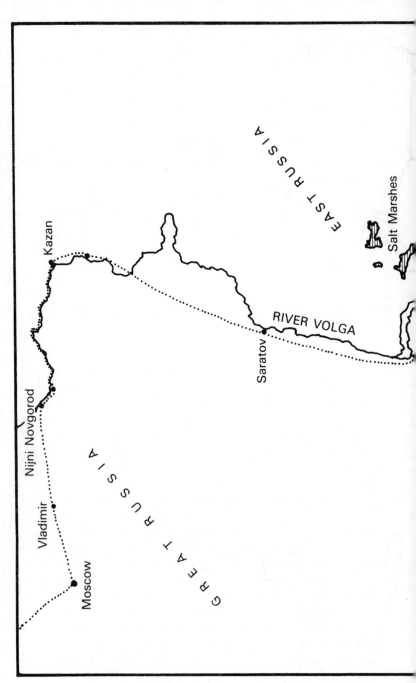

Anne Lister's route from Moscow to the Caucasus

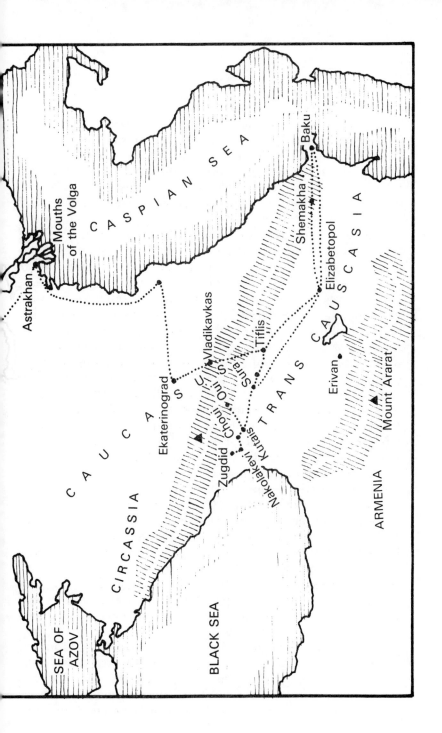

the English papers accounts of landslips, and burning forests at Saratoff. The former, over the Volga, are nothing to look at; they are like bits of slips at the back of the Isle of Wight — and as to the latter, it is probable incendiaries might not do more than the electric fluid and the excessive heat of the summer. The Moravian Sarepta contrasts strangely with the Calmuck village within the very precincts of the town. It was the first village we had seen of this half wild people with their felt tents, and fat-tailed sheep and goats all huddled together. About half way between Sarepta and Astrakhan, we stopt to see one of their capitals — a day's excursion across the Volga to Tumen — but the prince of Tumen headed a regiment of his Calmucks at the seige of Leipzig, and is an agreeable, gentlemanly man, proud of his descent from Ghenghiz Khan. His sister-in-law, a celebrated Calmuck beauty, did the honours; and, after attending their great service in the very handsome Chinese-like temple built by the present prince, we dined as we might have done *chez un prince Européen*. But how strange it seemed that such a man could still be pagan — could still revere Budda as his prophet, and the grand lama of Tibet as a divine incarnation! Our return (in the prince's equipage), galloping across the frozen Volga, with our wild looking horses, and the wild shouts of our Calmuck escort, was the most picturesque set-out I ever saw. The next day we came in for a large Calmuck fishing party on the Volga. The nets laid under the ice between two and three feet thick, were drawn up at an opening about a yard or two square — the great quantity of fish brought to mind the miracle-draught of a far other time and place. We bought, and ate of the fish on our arrival at Astrakhan in the evening, and never had we eaten anything more excellent of fish kind. Here we were in Asia. We saw the Hindoo worship — the town and neighbourhood boast not of beauty; but both are full of interest. The indigenes are principally Tatars. The Caspian being fifty miles off, and it not being possible to make a road anywhere near its shore (on account of reeds and marshes) we have seen a few of its inhabitants, but have not seen the sea itself, and were never nearer than within about twenty miles. From the Armenian cathedral at Kisliar we had the first view of the magnificent range of Caucasus, but the weather, tho' fine, was too nebulose to indulge us much till Ekaterinograd — from here, on a clear day, one can see the three great and highest summits, the Elbrus, Psamta, and Kasbek, the latter doubly interesting as being the giant of our route — the mountain-pass may be said to begin at Vladicavkas. The whole distance from there here, is about 120 English miles; and of these you may count about fifty to the point culminant. At the Pyrenees the transition from France to Spain is sufficiently striking; but here it is from Europe to Asia. I have neither time nor paper for description — but in interest, in improvement, in every advantage to be derived from foreign travel, my expectations are exceeded. We everywhere find an agreeable and polished society. A ball given by the commander in chief here (a very viceroy) is like a ball in London, or Paris, with the additional interest of Georgian beauty, and a picturesque mixture of Georgian costume with the *dernièrs modes de Paris*. In England, we know very little about Russia and still less of Georgia and its interesting capital. Those who have been here six or seven years ago, would hardly know the society and *artificial* features of the town again. The natural features are grand, and striking — a fine valley watered by the classic Kura at which Cyrus rested from his toil of conquest — a central point of architectural interest, and the very spot for a Walter Scott to light upon — Jason, the golden fleece, Medea, Circe, &c., &c., &c., and Ararat! We hope to be off on Saturday to the eternal fires of Baku. Our heads will be full of guibres, and naptha pits, and the dark blue wave of the treacherous Caspian. From there we propose making the best of our way to Erivan, paying our respects to the patriarch of all the Armenians, hoping he will be returned from his flock in Batavia (Dutch East Indies — no place so called hereabouts), and gazing on the *berceau* of mankind, the sacred Ararat, whose summit is too holy for human foot to tread again, according to Armenian belief which mocks the impiety of professor Parrot *cum multis aliis* (i.e. three or four more Europeans) who simply trust the evidence of their own senses, and affirm that they have reached the top. We shall gaze upon this, and drink the waters of the Araxes, and then make for the Phasis, and see what we can nearer here, and then, if we have time, which is doubtful, return by the Crimea. Direct your letter to the care of Messrs. A. Marc & Co. Moscow, Russia. I shall receive it *some* time, and will write to you again from *somewhere*. I shall, and do think of you often and affectionately. *Quant à tout ce qui regarde la vie amicale*, perhaps I am so little changed as most people, certainly much less than some that might be named if necessary, among whom I shall in future rank my dearest Mary if she does not place implicit faith in the ever affectionate regard &c., &c., &c., of her very affectionate friend

A.L. -

Monday night May 11. The post goes once a week — every Thursday. My letter was too late last week — we hope to be off tomorrow. The weather is delightful and we are impatient to be en route again — the horses ordered for seven in the morning. The distance from here to Baku is about 320 miles — we have seven or eight rivers to cross, and expect to be about six days on the road — on the eve of a journey one has always a thousand things to do. God bless you my dearest Mary!

18

FINALE

The account of Anne Lister's life and travels, as told in her letters, ends abruptly on August 7 1840, when she was at Nakolakevi. Her journal, however, continued to August 11, and tells how the two travellers left the Palace of Prince Bijan Dadian early on August 8, and continued on horse-back to Zugdidi, where they spent the night. The next day they lunched and dined with Prince and Princess Dadian and met there the French botanist, M. Liétaud.

The journey was continued through Liia, where a rather disturbed night was spent:

August 11. Awakened last night between one and two, cats at my cheese, and children squalling enough to distract the old gentleman himself. A(dny) awoke me before six, anxious to be off. She ordered the horses ... So many women and people knew not whom to give to — gave nothing. The cot(tage)s so hid among the trees and vines and eight foot high maize, hardly visible except when close upon them. Off at six fifty. The children especially, and the men and women, look pale and yellow and unhealthy in this moist hot bot(tom) (valley?).

The same day Djkali was reached, and the two Englishwomen slept in the corn barn (a little wicker place about four and a half by three yards in size). Here the diary ends, and all that is known of Miss Lister's subsequent life is that she was at Lailache (Letchakoum) on 31 August, and that she died near Tiflis in Georgia, of a violent fever, on 22 September 1840, aged forty-nine years. The only light that can be thrown on the early death of this intrepid Yorkshirewoman is the information given in the following notices from *The Halifax Guardian*.

Halifax Guardian. 31 October 1840.

Deaths.

On Tuesday September 22, at Koutais, of '*La fièvre chaude*',
Mrs Lister, of Shibden Hall, Halifax, Yorkshire.

Local intelligence.
The late Miss Lister of Shibden Hall.
In our obituary this week we regret to record the name of this respected and lamented lady, whose benefactions to our charitable and religious institutions will long be remembered, and whose public spirit in the improvement of our town and neighbourhood is attested by lasting memorials. In mental energy and courage she resembled Lady Mary Wortley Montague and Lady Hester Stanhope; and, like these celebrated women, after exploring Europe she extended her researches to those oriental regions, where her career has been so prematurely terminated. We are informed that the remains of this distinguished lady have been embalmed, and that her friend and companion, Miss Walker, is bringing them home by way of Constantinople, for interment in the family vault. She died near Tiflis, but within the Circassian border. Miss Lister was descended from an ancient family in Lancashire, the main branch of which is represented by the noble line of Ribblesdale.

Halifax Guardian. 1 May 1841.

The late Mrs Lister. The remains of this lady (who, our readers will remember died at Koutais, in Imerethi, on September 22 last) arrived at Shibden Hall late on Saturday night, and were interred in the parish church, on Thursday morning.

INDEX